Dyslexia and Working Memory

Drawing on decades of expertise alongside a large dataset of assessment results, this book offers an integrated, lifespan perspective on dyslexia and its lasting effects. It reframes dyslexia as an information processing difficulty, with working-memory weakness at its core, leading to cognitive overload in learning, work, and everyday life. Aimed at individuals with dyslexia as well as educators, coaches, counsellors, and career advisors, the authors provide practical, evidence-based recommendations for managing associated challenges, with a particular focus on strategy development and the use of assistive technology. Bridging neuroscience, cognitive psychology, and educational psychology, the text promotes scientific understanding of dyslexia in all its manifestations.

DAVID MCLOUGHLIN is a registered educational and occupational psychologist. He is Director of the Independent Dyslexia Consultants, London, UK, as well as Professor of Professional Practice at the University of Buckingham. He has conducted thousands of differential assessments for both children and adults during a career of more than 50 years.

ALAN MARTIN is a chartered psychologist and former Dean of the School of Psychology at the University of Buckingham. He has carried out assessments with adults in education and employment at the Independent Dyslexia Consultants, London, UK, for over 15 years.

Dyslexia and Working Memory

A Scientific and Practical Lifespan Perspective

DAVID MCLOUGHLIN
University of Buckingham

ALAN MARTIN
University of Buckingham

CAMBRIDGE
UNIVERSITY PRESS

Shaftesbury Road, Cambridge CB2 8EA, United Kingdom

One Liberty Plaza, 20th Floor, New York, NY 10006, USA

477 Williamstown Road, Port Melbourne, VIC 3207, Australia

314–321, 3rd Floor, Plot 3, Splendor Forum, Jasola District Centre,
New Delhi – 110025, India

103 Penang Road, #05-06/07, Visioncrest Commercial, Singapore 238467

Cambridge University Press is part of Cambridge University Press & Assessment, a department of the University of Cambridge.

We share the University's mission to contribute to society through the pursuit of education, learning and research at the highest international levels of excellence.

www.cambridge.org
Information on this title: www.cambridge.org/9781009282659

DOI: 10.1017/9781009282628

© David McLoughlin and Alan Martin 2026

This publication is in copyright. Subject to statutory exception and to the provisions of relevant collective licensing agreements, no reproduction of any part may take place without the written permission of Cambridge University Press & Assessment.

When citing this work, please include a reference to the DOI 10.1017/9781009282628

First published 2026

A catalogue record for this publication is available from the British Library

A Cataloging-in-Publication data record for this book is available from the Library of Congress

ISBN 978-1-009-28265-9 Hardback
ISBN 978-1-009-28263-5 Paperback

Cambridge University Press & Assessment has no responsibility for the persistence or accuracy of URLs for external or third-party internet websites referred to in this publication and does not guarantee that any content on such websites is, or will remain, accurate or appropriate.

For EU product safety concerns, contact us at Calle de José Abascal, 56, 1°, 28003 Madrid, Spain, or email eugpsr@cambridge.org

We are grateful to Kellie Bolger, our personal assistant, who through her diligence and humour manages our cognitive load and helps us keep our working memories functioning.

David and Alan

Contents

List of Figures	*page*	viii
List of Tables		ix
Preface		xi

1	Dyslexia across the Life Course: A Scientific Perspective	1
2	Definitions and Models of Dyslexia	13
3	Evidence from Practice	34
4	Working Memory	65
5	Rapid Naming	79
6	Making Memory Work	87
7	Working Memory and Performance Improvement	96
8	Working Memory and Counselling	112
9	Working Memory and Career Development	123
	Conclusion	139
	Appendix	144
	References	149
	Index	167

Figures

3.1	The structure of the WAIS-IV assessment showing indices and associated subtests.	*page* 39
3.2	WAIS-IV conceptual structure.	44
3.3	WAIS-IV hierarchical structure.	45
3.4	Sample mean scores of the WAIS-IV subtests (with 95% CI).	49
3.5	Sample mean scores of the WAIS-IV subtests (with standard deviation error bars).	51
3.6	Sample mean scores for the WAIS-IV subtests comparing the education (university) and employment (work) groups.	54
A.1	Mean index scores for the Chapter 3 sample (with 95% CI).	144
A.2	Mean WAIS index scores for the Chapter 3 sample (with one standard deviation error range).	144
A.3	Bar charts showing the mean index scores by client type, those in higher education (university) and those in employment (with 95% CI).	145
A.4	Bar charts showing the mean index scores by client type, those in higher education (university) and those in employment (1 SD).	145
A.5	Bar charts showing the mean subtest scores by client type, those in higher education (university) and those in employment (work). The error bars depict standard deviations.	146

Tables

3.1	Correlations between the 10 subtest scores of the WAIS-IV (letter-number sequencing rather than arithmetic) within the adult dyslexic client sample.	*page* 53
3.2	Factor analysis pattern matrix of the 10 WAIS-IV subtests for the sample of dyslexic clients.	58
3.3	Correlations between the three oblique factors extracted from the dyslexic client sample.	59
3.4	Correlations between the rapid-naming measures.	60
3.5	Correlations between the literacy skill measures.	60
3.6	Correlations between the rapid-naming measures and the literacy skill measures.	62
A.1	Statistical appendices.	147

Preface

The authors of this book are psychologists, trained according to the scientist practitioner approach to interventions, and influenced by the empiricist tradition. We adopt this approach when conducting diagnostic evaluations, as well as when making recommendations as to how individuals might be supported in education, training, and the workplace. In this book we have taken a scientific viewpoint, mindful that Popper's criteria for this are testability and refutability (Popper, 1963). The results of research that does not meet one of these are pseudoscience. Unfortunately, there has been a great deal of the latter in the field of neurodevelopmental disorders, leading to inappropriate terminology that confuses rather than clarifies, assessment methodologies that humiliate rather than inform, and interventions that promise much and heighten expectations, but do not work.

As well as the data from our records described here, we have relied on published research in neuroscience, cognitive psychology, and education, wherever possible from the twenty-first century. This has all contributed to the understanding of neurodevelopmental disorders, none more so than dyslexia. Unfortunately, there is little integration of findings or inference to the potential impact beyond reading. Dyslexia is neurobiological in origin, and this is acknowledged in the International Classification of Diseases 11 (ICD-11) (World Health Organization, 2022). Neurological differences have an impact on cognitive functions, with consequent effects for learning and performance. It is time for more collaboration amongst researchers so that dyslexia can be better understood in its many manifestations across the lifespan. To achieve that, we have tried here to integrate empirical findings from the different disciplines so that assessments and interventions are evidence based. Generalisations from the experiences of the few are not sufficient. We do not consider dyslexia to be a gift or a superpower, but a cognitive inefficiency that undermines the acquisition of skills, effective learning, and performance. It makes life more demanding for people with dyslexia than it is for others through no fault of their own. They deserve better than pseudoscience, myth, pop psychology, and internecine academic debate.

1 Dyslexia across the Life Course: A Scientific Perspective

INTRODUCTION

More than 25 years ago, Miles et al. (1998) described dyslexia as a syndrome that persists across the lifespan and shows itself in many other ways than poor reading. This remark sums up our perspective on dyslexia and the philosophy behind this book. We understand dyslexia to be a neurologically based syndrome – a group of symptoms including problems with reading, writing, spelling, and the procedural aspects of maths. These are the behavioural markers associated with an underlying information-processing problem related to academic skills, but we argue that the neurological basis has a considerable impact on wider areas of functioning.

As psychologists, both authors have extensive experience of conducting diagnostic evaluations for people who are finding aspects of life more demanding than they are for others. Sometimes they are individuals we have tested before, so we are in the unique position of seeing how the syndrome continues to manifest itself across the life course. Our opening question is usually 'why do you want this assessment now?' Those who are hoping to understand themselves better and not just seeking access to resources and adjustments refer to inconsistencies in their performance, specific examples being:

'I have always seemed to work harder than my friends, but they get better results.'
'I can't remember people's names.'
'I can't tell left from right.'
'I am always late.'
'I read slowly.'
'I can't remember what I have read.'

'My spelling is awful.'
'I run out of time in tests.'
'I find it difficult to follow conversations when more than one person is speaking.'
'I can tell people what I think but can't put it on paper.'

We are interested in what creates these difficulties, not only because it is fascinating but also because it can help those of us who advise people with dyslexia improve their lives. We can think of causes as either proximate or ultimate. We know that problems with reading do not have a simple cause (a causes b), and that often a range of factors is involved. When we refer to an ultimate cause, such as the neurological basis for dyslexia, it is to attempt to identify its origin, in this case one based in material reality, something that can be measured in the brain. A proximate cause can be thought of as something just prior to the outcome, such as a problem with reading. In this case it can be the group of symptoms we call dyslexia, and then we assume it is the ultimate cause of the person's difficulties.

If we make a mistake in attribution, it can have detrimental effects on our clients. For example, if we treat dyslexia as the ultimate cause of the reader's difficulty, then it will depend on, for example, which definition of dyslexia we use. If that definition of dyslexia only includes reference to problems with reading accuracy and fluency, then we reach a tautological situation in which the very problem we are seeking an explanation for is repeated back to us. Question: 'Why do you have trouble with reading?' Response: 'Because I have dyslexia.' Question: 'What does that mean?' Response: 'I have trouble with reading.' This is not an unusual conversation with clients, but academic writers do not make it any clearer. In a commentary on the International Dyslexia Association (IDA) definition of dyslexia Elliot and Grigorenko (2024) recommend that dyslexia should be defined as 'a severe and persistent difficulty in accurate and fluent reading' (p. 10). So, the answer to the question 'why do people have trouble with reading?' becomes 'because they have a problem with reading'. Finding ultimate explanations can be challenging, but if we understand them, we can start to realise that we cannot yet change a person's neurological structure, but given an understanding of the outcomes that result from this, we can advise on strategies they can use to work around their difficulties.

It has been suggested that of all learning disorders dyslexia is best understood (Pennington et al., 2019). In the ensuing chapters it will be evident that this is true to some extent, but it will also be clear that there is much misunderstanding. There is little consensus concerning definition, muddled language, and confusion between correlation and cause. The much-cited Rose Review prepared in the United Kingdom defined dyslexia as 'a learning difficulty that primarily affects the skills involved in accurate and fluent word reading and spelling. Characteristic features of dyslexia are difficulties in phonological awareness, verbal memory, and verbal processing speed. Dyslexia occurs across the range of intellectual abilities' (Rose, 2009, p. 10). We will return to the last sentence later but point out here that it is contrary to the original notion of specificity. The latter acknowledges that individuals have mostly average to better-than-average intellectual abilities, but have cognitive weaknesses in areas that undermine performance and differentiate those who have specific disorders such as dyslexia from those who have a general learning disability (Kirk, 1962). A person who has a general learning disability will show some of the characteristics associated with dyslexia, particularly involving information processing, but they will also have many more problems. If all we do is focus on the difficulties linked to dyslexia, we cannot distinguish between the general and the specific. Essentially, it is the difference between people who have trouble learning some things and those who have trouble learning most things. To suggest that people experience the latter raises expectations that they will not be able to fulfil and is contrary to the effort that has been made to disassociate dyslexia from low intelligence. The Rose Review definition also confuses skills and abilities. The former are empirically traceable behavioural performances that are about application rather than abilities. The latter are cognitive capabilities that are theoretical constructs, so cognition is not necessarily about application (Scerri & Will, 2023). Reading and spelling are skills, things that can be learned, acquired, and taught. Phonological awareness, verbal memory, and verbal processing speed are abilities. They are innate, probably not teachable, although they can be addressed through strategy development. The simplest model is that our skills are built upon the foundation of our abilities.

The literal meaning of dyslexia from Greek is a difficulty with words. One of the early pioneers in the field (Critchley, 1981) acknowledged that dyslexia is a difficulty in the use of words, how they are identified, what they signify, and how they are handled in combination, pronounced, and spelled (p. 2). He considered it to be more than a reading or spelling problem. Snowling (2014) wrote that 'current evidence places dyslexia on a continuum with other language impairments' (p. 43). More recently, studies have revealed that even high-achieving individuals with dyslexia can have impaired oral language skills (Bradshaw et al., 2021). At the least, therefore, we need to consider dyslexia to have an impact on both verbal and written language skills.

Consider how we learn to use language in all human societies. Almost everyone learns to produce language, unless there are neurodevelopmental reasons for them being unable to do so. This most often involves the production and comprehension of abstract sounds, but it can also involve visual communication in the form of sign language. It typically begins in the second year of life (late infancy) with single words and develops rapidly into multi-word sentences. This development has the appearance of automaticity because we can observe that children are not explicitly taught to speak. We understand now that from birth, and possibly before, infants are acquiring an understanding of the fundamental building blocks of their native language: the phonemes (sounds) and grammar (structure). In developmental psychology it is said that comprehension precedes production, that children often know and understand much more than they can demonstrate. This is certainly the case with the ability that is language learning.

Contrast this with literacy learning. No one has ever learned to read and write passively. It is an active process that involves linking the phonemes and the grammar of the language to a visual form. It is reversible in that we call writing encoding and reading decoding. The 'coding' part is important because this is the written form of the language, and symbolism is so fundamental to humans that we have been referred to as *Homo Symbolicus* (Deacon, 1998). Literacy skill development is active and difficult, but it is built upon language ability. It is a complicated skill to acquire because it has multiple sub-skills, including the phonological, orthographic, and semantic levels of language (Seidenberg, 2017).

People with dyslexia display inconsistencies; we still do not know enough about the frequency of these or the extent to which they fall outside what Kahneman has called 'the valley of the normal' in which there are no surprises or inconsistencies (Kahneman et al., 2021). There are insufficient contemporary large-scale surveys addressing their occurrence, either amongst the general population or those who have identified specific learning disorders such as dyslexia. Too much research relies on qualitative data, often referred to as 'lived experience'. We can learn much from the insider perspective (Reiff et al., 1993) but must acknowledge that it is just that, and individuals' experiences, both positive and negative, will vary greatly and cannot be tested or refuted. It belongs to identity theory, the narrative being an internalised story created about oneself or one's personal myth (McAdams, 2011). Personal stories 'are understandable, memorable and naturally integrated with intuitive reasoning. They are more compelling than statistics' (Redelmeier et al., 2025, p. 5). Dressing up lived experience as phenomenology (Pathak, 2017) does not improve matters as the nature of the latter is that it 'finds things' and is subject to confirmation bias. Even one of the bellwethers of phenomenology, Jean-Paul Sartre (1971), acknowledged that it will never converge with empirical science. It belongs to philosophy rather than scientific psychology. Relying on description and definition by the activist core and the disgruntled will not do (see, for example,

Cameron, 2024). It has been suggested that postmodernists' arguments for reducing uncertainty or approximating truth are apparently non-existent, and their method of reducing uncertainty seems to rely solely on the supposed truth of personal experience or authoritative pronouncements. The aphorism 'the plural of anecdote is not data' should be acknowledged when considering reports of qualitative research, as they can misinform. At best, 'lived experience' might generate hypotheses that can be tested through systematic empirical studies. Anyone who has spoken to an adult who has dyslexia could not exclude the impact on spelling from its description and definition. It is often the problem they identify as having caused them the most embarrassment.

In distinguishing between science and pseudoscience, Popper (1963) argues that the criterion for the former is its falsifiability. That is, a scientific theory should be testable, and it should be clear how it could be disproven. The perceptions of the experiences of individuals cannot be refuted. In schema that have been developed to rate the quality of research on which evidence-based practice should rely, lived experience research is the lowest (West et al., 2002). In addition, and possibly more dangerously, the accusations of those holding these views that any questioning of their 'theories' is ableist, colonialist, supremacist, or whichever 'ist' is currently most fashionable on social media seeks to end debate, inquiry, and the discovery of ultimate causes that could help people with dyslexia and other specific learning disorders. It has been suggested that the implications of cultural and cognitive relativism have been severe, negative, and poisonous for the field of special education (Kauffman & Sasso, 2006).

MODELS IN SCIENCE AND PSYCHOLOGY

It has become commonplace to refer to science as if it is a body of irrefutable knowledge, whereas it is a method or process. It operates on models of reality, theoretical concepts that attempt to account for phenomena and in the case of psychology explain behaviour or atleast establish probable causality. Theories only predict probabilities and should be supported by and refined based on data from systematic research. Rovelli (2018) wrote that 'we need to adapt our philosophy to our science, and not our science to our philosophy' (p. 118). Scientists conjecture ideas and consider their refutation. Immanuel Kant has been paraphrased as writing that 'concepts without data are empty; data without concepts are blind' (Guyer & Wood, 1998). It is suggested here that the continued focus on skills such as reading accuracy has led to research findings becoming data without a concept.

Dyslexia research has gathered findings related to reading without consideration of the bigger picture. It is driven by the pressures in modern academia to produce 'output' that will help achieve personal and institutional goals linked to publication counts. 'Publishing in higher-tier journals is easier when the story is simple, and doing so can quickly turn into a citation goldmine if the field invests in challenging your theory' (Astle & Fletcher-Watson, 2020, p. 242). The pressure to publish might also account for the contrary opinions concerning dyslexia espoused by the same author in different papers and books. Much research is confirmatory, results supporting existing theories concerning the cognitive abilities associated with literacy. The notion of a core-deficit persists, a weakness in phonological processing being thought to be the cause of reading accuracy problems, confusing correlation with causation. The latter implies the former, and its 'contrast with mere correlation is the lifeblood of science' (Pinker, 2022, p. 246). Furthermore, there has been insufficient inference as to how the cognitive processes associated with reading might have an impact on other aspects of behaviour, leading to pseudoscientific notions of types of dyslexia such as 'naming dyslexia', referring to word-finding problems, 'directional dyslexia', which describes being unable to distinguish between left and right, and 'stealth dyslexia', referring to hidden difficulties that are not evident until demands increase at times of transition. Even within reading research it has been suggested that we should distinguish between specific reading comprehension deficit (S-RCD) and dyslexia

(Barquero & Cutting, 2021). If dyslexia is reframed as a problem with information processing, the links with literacy skills become clearer, and other difficulties make more sense within the context of what we already know.

Although it is usually referred to as developmental dyslexia, the emphasis on reading research has often failed to acknowledge the 'developmental' aspect, that is, human beings' neurological, cognitive, emotional, intellectual, and social capabilities over the course of a usual lifespan. Even if we just focus on reading, it is important to acknowledge neuroplasticity, changes in cognition, as well as different stages and demands. From preschool age to eight years, children are learning to read. Between ages 8 and 11, they should be reading to learn. In adolescence, reading skills should be established so a student can learn how to learn, and in adulthood they should be independent learners. The cognitive weaknesses associated with dyslexia and their consequent behavioural expression are therefore of significance at different ages, so research has not sufficiently reflected the broader perspective advanced by Miles. For example, phonological awareness 'seems to be a minor problem in adulthood' (Reis et al., 2020, p. 365). It might be important when a child is learning to read, but not when as an adult the same person is trying to understand and absorb complex material associated with a course of study or occupation. In a recent edition of the *Oxford Review of Education* devoted to dyslexia, Miles' work is eulogised in one paper (Evans, 2020), but definitions in others are still focused on literacy, particularly word decoding and spelling fluency (Snowling et al., 2020). Furthermore, in an American paper titled 'Solving the problem of learning disabilities' (Siegel, 2019), it was suggested that what is required to confirm whether or not somebody has a learning disability such as dyslexia is to assess their reading, spelling, mathematics, and perhaps writing. In other words, to just establish behavioural characteristics such as academic attainments, without reference to the cognitive-processing difficulties that are neurologically based and undermine the acquisition of skills beyond literacy and numeracy.

The real problem with 'learning disabilities' is 'learning' and the focus on academic skills. Successful people with dyslexia often learn very well but have worked harder at developing skills and rely on means others do not have to depend upon. They are often inappropriately described as 'compensated dyslexics', but this only refers to reading accuracy and has been an unconscious rather than a deliberate process. It is their *performance* in academic skills that is undermined, not their ability to learn. The criterion of poor reading, it has been argued, can only be applied between the ages of 5 and 14 years because a child can't be a poor reader before the former, and by young adolescence many can read adequately even though they did not start well. Miles et al. (1998) wrote that 'it would make for better communication if those who want to limit their studies to reading did not use the word dyslexia at all' (p. 48). Nevertheless, the focus on literacy persists, for example, Snowling et al. (2020) proposed that the term dyslexia should only be used to refer to a difficulty with decoding and spelling fluency that is persistent over time and affects academic functioning in literacy-based areas of the curriculum. Further, in a recent paper that attempts to clarify the conceptualisation of dyslexia, the emphasis remains on the acquisition of accurate and/or fluent reading, spelling, and comprehension (Wolf et al., 2024).

The focus here is a lifelong perspective, as it is only when we acknowledge that syndromes such as dyslexia persist throughout life, not necessarily at a literacy level but as a processing difficulty that undermines a range of skills extending beyond the academic, that we will come to understand them. There is, therefore, a need for conceptual models of dyslexia that address all its manifestations, especially as there has always been a socio-political agenda surrounding the concept, and inevitably in the United Kingdom some of the criticism is class based. Journalists and politicians, usually 'critics with a credo' to use a phrase from Auden (2005), have questioned the concept. Much of this has been based on a misunderstanding of nuanced debates about reading difficulties, leading to the conclusion that 'dyslexia does not exist', the work of academics opposed to the concept that emphasises disagreement cited in support (Elliott & Grigorenko, 2014, 2024), whereas a theory should rest on evidence in favour of it, not just evidence against it (Shermer, 2018). Rather than improve the understanding of those who find life more demanding than others, the consequence has been the denial of resources and increased anxiety amongst people with dyslexia.

Based on the existing scientific literature and an analysis of our archive data, it is our view that dyslexia's ultimate cause is an inherited neurological inefficiency resulting from differences in brain structure and connectivity that leads to a significant deficit in the information-processing ability known as working memory (see Chapters 3 and 4). The overwhelming evidence for this proposition derives from work with children as well as adults and helps explain why this persisting weakness in working memory has a significant impact on literacy skills, as well as other behaviours.

LABELS

Many papers have been devoted to the use of labels in the field of learning disorders and often adopt a negative perspective, suggesting that they can undermine self-efficacy beliefs (Jodrell, 2010), but 'we cannot avoid labels because we must have words to describe things, including the characteristics of the people we encounter' (Kauffman, 2007, p. 246). Contrary to the postmodernist rejection of the idea that words cannot refer to anything, we accept that if something has a name it exists, and our world is defined by the words we use. A word 'gives origin to all things' (Momaday, 1987, p. 33). We might argue about their nature and should refine meaning according to increased understanding. Regarding dyslexia, the much-cited adage 'the absence of evidence is not evidence of absence' (Sagan & Druyan, 1997, p. 213) certainly applies. 'Science is not reliable because it provides certainty. It is reliable because it provides us with the best answers we have at present' (Rovelli, 2018, p. 232). The objective data from neuroscience and cognitive science that helps us understand dyslexia in all its manifestations has grown substantially and is increasing all the time

(Ramus, 2014). It cannot be ignored, but if research findings are to make sense, clarification of the concept is necessary.

Dyslexia, unlike terms for general learning disorders, has avoided what has been termed the *euphemism treadmill* (Pinker, 2003) of constantly changing terms for the same core concept. However, this has not prevented dyslexia itself being categorised under a range of different labels such as 'challenged', 'gifted', and 'neurodiverse'. People with dyslexia experience difficulties that are ultimately due to them having lower-functioning working-memory capacity because of neurological differences. They are not challenged, dyslexia being an inherent product of their neurology, not an external factor, although the demands of education and employment highlight their difficulties. They are not gifted because they have dyslexia, although they may well be gifted despite it. They are no more or less diverse than any other group of people; however, they are *distinct* in the ultimate cause of their difficulty. Kauffman (2007, p. 246) has written that:

> People soon figure out the euphemisms we use for the phenomena we call disabilities, failure, or superior achievement. Referring to a disability as a challenge sets up people with disabilities for eventual ridicule. Euphemisms fool no one for very long, but they do confuse communication for a while and ultimately make whatever we are referring to appear more negative or less worthy of respect than the original term.

We do not need new language and terminology but a clarification of what we mean by dyslexia, its origins and impact, if we are to help people find solutions and work towards achieving their academic, occupational, and life goals.

SUMMARY

The main points of this chapter, in which we have established the tone for the rest of this book, include:

- questioning the continued focus of dyslexia research on reading;
- placing dyslexia within the context of it being a neurodevelopmental disorder;
- stressing that dyslexia has an impact on cognitive functioning, so it is a broader syndrome that affects many behaviours;
- promoting an empirical, evidence-based approach to understanding and defining dyslexia that explains all the inconsistencies in a person's performance;
- emphasising a lifelong perspective;
- criticising the use of euphemisms to refer to learning disorders such as dyslexia rather that clarifying the concept.

2 Definitions and Models of Dyslexia

INTRODUCTION

Anastasiou (2024) has written that the field of specific learning disabilities has faced three kinds of challenges: *constitutional*, which arise from historical conceptualisations, definitions, and theoretical constructs; *internal*, which relate to the inherent difficulties involved in conducting scientific research; and *external*, including ideological movements such as social constructivism and social trends such as neurodiversity. We address all three implicitly and explicitly in this chapter.

THE PROBLEM OF DEFINITION

Definitions provide theoretical models that can be tested, but defining dyslexia adequately has continued to be a controversial matter. It should remain so as we understand more about the syndrome, but this should not just be a subject for academic debate as it has consequences for diagnosis, as well as resulting interventions. The focus of research has largely continued to be literacy skills, mainly reading, and the understanding of dyslexia has been impeded by the emphasis on these.

There are three main approaches to defining and identifying dyslexia: discrepancy, profile of strengths and weaknesses (PSW), and response to intervention (RTI). Each has its flaws, and none are adequate if we take a long-term perspective. We focus here on the first two as RTI relies on the progress students make following changes in teaching. It has its advocates (Gibbs & Elliott, 2020) and has become very popular in primary or elementary education, but is not relevant when there is a late diagnosis, which is often the case for adolescents and adults, where there has been no intervention to respond to. Response to intervention is a 'wait and see how badly they fail' method. The risk is that if changes are made and the individual continues to struggle, by the time the nature of their difficulties is understood and they have appropriate support, emotional issues can arise. They will have lost confidence in their ability and experience anxiety, exacerbating their problems with learning and performance. It is easier to help someone find ways around poor spelling than it is to re-establish confidence once it has been undermined.

Discrepancy Definitions

It is 'a sense of incongruity' that should lead to speculation that someone might have a learning disorder such as dyslexia (Miles, 1983). This has been formalised, and traditionally, but controversially, diagnosticians have relied on discrepancy definitions, adopting them as criteria for the diagnosis of dyslexia, the discrepancy being between expected performance and achievement, usually reading accuracy. They have fallen out of favour, although Snowling et al. (2020) have argued for their return. Nonetheless, Siegel et al. (2022) have remained critical, arguing that 'both empirically and practically, the use of discrepancy criteria for dyslexia identification is not supported' (p. 53). The International Classification of Diseases 11 (ICD-11), for example, is based on a discrepancy definition, although it extends beyond reading accuracy to include skills such as fluency and comprehension, areas in which people continue to have difficulties throughout life. In ICD-11 (World Health Organization, 2022) dyslexia is described as 'a developmental learning disorder with impairment in reading'. That its origin is largely genetic but that environmental factors modulate its effects is acknowledged. ICD-11 also considers ability: not everyone is average in terms of their intellectual abilities, and it is nonsense to discount the levels one could be expected to achieve based on these. The notion of the irrelevance of ability tests is often promoted by individuals who have little understanding of their utility. The Rose Report (2009) refers to dyslexia occurring across a range of levels of intellectual ability, thereby negating the notion of it being a specific disorder. It is assumed here that the general intelligence of people with dyslexia ranges from the low average to the very high. Verbal and non-verbal reasoning abilities are not affected by a neurodevelopmental disorder such as dyslexia (Callens et al., 2014). Clarifying persisting misconceptions that associate dyslexia with a lack of intelligence, potential to learn, or talents has been described as of critical importance in defining dyslexia (Wolf et al., 2024).

Discrepancy definitions highlight some of the inconsistencies in a person's performance. Relying on specific criteria such as those outlined in ICD-11 for different learning disorders can also facilitate a move away from the package approach to diagnosis in which assessors follow a recommended protocol, regardless of the issues that have been raised. It is not unusual to see reports of diagnostic assessments during which tests have been administered just because they are on a prescribed list. They include reference to definitions that have been cobbled together by advocacy groups and committees that attempt to please everyone and confuse symptoms, causes, and correlations. There needs to be more differentiation, addressing the questions of what someone is finding difficult and why that might be the case. The process is known as differential diagnosis, and when conducted properly it can resolve some of the issues surrounding the poorly understood notion of co-morbidity or co-occurrence at a behavioural level. Sometimes assessors include checklists for other syndromes such as attention deficit disorder (ADD) or attention deficit hyperactivity disorder (ADHD), dyspraxia, and specific visual difficulties, regardless of whether symptoms of these have been noted. There is a trade-off between carrying out lengthy testing, using an all-inclusive battery where the risk is that some of the testing is irrelevant, and carrying out an informed and targeted evaluation based upon an individual's reported difficulties. The former complicates the diagnostic process, fails to promote understanding, and overloads the client with testing, which can lead to inaccurate results. Reliance on schemas such as ICD-11 can contribute to a better understanding of co-morbidity as there are clear criteria for different syndromes. Generic assessments lead to generic solutions, the guidance relating to interventions being 'one size fits all', whereas consultation with the client to establish what they are finding difficult can provide the assessment with a focus and address their questions.

One of the fundamental problems with discrepancy definitions is that, if we take a lifespan perspective, what should we consider at a skill level? Adults require the skills they need to live their daily lives, pursue formal education and training, and carry out the tasks necessary to a particular occupation. There are few if any formal measures of the last, most tests being designed for educational purposes, thus there is a need for criterion referencing that addresses whether people have the skills and abilities required for a particular job. Furthermore, even if we agree on what should be included, there is a faux science or pretence at objectivity, cut-off points being arbitrary and often based on policy determined by the availability of resources rather than need.

Profile of Strengths and Weaknesses (PSW)

Noting incongruities or discrepancies in performance is fundamental to the notion of the specificity of learning disorders. It is not, however, sufficient, as these need to be explained.

If we focus on cognition rather than behavioural characteristics such as reading, the most useful diagnostic model that also defines dyslexia is the profile of strengths and weaknesses (PSW). It has been described as 'the only empirically based approach that attempts to identify the pattern of deficit in the basic psychological processes that interfere with academic achievement' (Fiorello et al., 2014, p. 55). The model was developed for use with children but can be applied across the lifespan. It is consistent with the original notion of learning disorders such as dyslexia in which specificity and variation were major tenets (see, for example, Bannatyne, 1974). Practitioners have adopted a PSW approach without a knowledge of the background to the concept of specific learning disorders, whereas all historic approaches have emphasised the 'spared or intact abilities that stand in stark contrast to the deficient abilities' (Kauffman, 2007, p. 7). The concept of cognitive specificity is not new and has been retained in ICD-11. There is, for example, a history of identifying profiles on the Wechsler intelligence scales that relate to specific learning disorders, including the ACID profile (arithmetic, coding, information, and digit span) associated with dyslexia, and the SCAD profile (symbol search, coding, arithmetic, and digit span) linked to ADD/ADHD (see Zhu & Weiss, 2005, for discussion). Terminology that belongs to pop psychology such as a 'spiky profile' (Isaacs, 2019; Doyle, 2020) that has been adopted does not advance scientific understanding, although it has already become part of the folklore associated with developmental learning disorders. It is only based on the cognitive profiles associated with a specific test, the Wechsler scales, not the population at large. The results described in Chapter 3 reveal profiles of strengths and weakness, but only for a sample of individuals using particular tests.

Essentially, the PSW approach is based on establishing that there is an academic or work-related issue that can be explained by cognitive weaknesses that have an evidence-based link to the specific areas of underperformance. Rose (2009) acknowledged that characteristics or features of dyslexia are difficulties in phonological processing, verbal memory, and processing speed, but we reiterate that this confuses symptoms with contributing factors. The data presented in Chapter 3 of this book demonstrates that individuals experiencing learning and performance difficulties manifest a profile of competencies and weaknesses. The competencies such as verbal abilities have been shown to be correlated with a range of skills important to effective functioning in educational and work settings. These also eliminate the possibility of an individual having a general learning disability. Most of us would do better on some subtests of an ability scale than on others. It is only when an ipsative approach to analysing test scores, comparing individuals with themselves, is adopted and some scores are well below their own average that there will be a substantial impact on performance. The starting point in the PSW approach is establishing that statistically significant scale score differences between competencies and processing abilities exist. Methods for doing so are integral to tests such as the Wechsler scales (see Lichtenberger & Kaufman, 2012). Understanding the pattern of strengths and weaknesses an individual manifests is essential to developing their self-understanding, ensuring that they can make informed decisions about their future, as well as become proactive in finding the best strategies and solutions. We should be considering a combination of discrepancies and profiles of strengths and weaknesses. Internecine arguments about the best approach to definition and diagnosis do little to assist individuals with dyslexia, and, as with all polarised debates, compromise is needed. Turner (2008) achieved this when he described two principal criteria for dyslexia:

1. An unexpected underachievement in one or more basic skill area (reading, spelling, arithmetic, comprehension);
2. Positive evidence of inefficiency in the management of information, for instance in short-term memory.

If we take a lifetime perspective, the first criterion should be widened to include performance generally: academic, work-related, and life skills. It is not always possible to measure these objectively. Needing to work harder than one's peers might be subjective, but a judgement might be made based on the competencies demonstrated through testing. The second needs to include more of the processing abilities that recent research has shown to be associated with skills and achievement such as working memory and executive functions. What might be challenging can be inferred from weaknesses in these. The person who has low working-memory capacity will, for example, need to work harder at and take longer over tasks that depend on it.

THE SCIENCE OF DYSLEXIA

As Pennington et al. (2019) have suggested, of all the learning disorders, dyslexia is the best understood. We know the most about its developmental neuropsychology, we have converging results regarding its structural and functional brain phenotype, and considerable progress has been made regarding its aetiology. It can be understood at biological, cognitive, and behavioural levels. The framework described by Frith (1999) remains a helpful way of organising what we know. It refers to differences at three levels:

1. biological differences: genetics and neurology;
2. cognitive differences: information processing;
3. observed behavioural differences such as in reading, writing, and spelling.

We begin here with the last of the three and then address the matter of explanation by reference to biology and cognition.

Behavioural Differences

The children included in the samples on which many early explanatory studies and theories were based are now adults. There is a growing academic literature that reports the findings of investigations into the symptoms of dyslexia manifested in the adult years. Studies vary in sample size, theoretical perspectives on dyslexia, as well as research methodologies. Many are based on easily accessed populations such as university students. Listed here are some of the findings. They are reported uncritically but are referenced at the end of the book so readers can form their own opinions as to validity, reliability, and the extent to which results can be generalised.

In follow-up to reading disability research conducted in the 1970s known as the Isle of Wight study, Maughan et al. (2009) found that adults:

- could read accurately, albeit laboriously;
- continued to experience problems with skills such as reading comprehension;
- found spelling difficult;
- had trouble organising ideas on paper.

Meta-analytic studies (Swanson & Hsieh, 2009; Moojen et al., 2020; Reis et al., 2020) have shown that adults with dyslexia have trouble with:

- many activities that rely on the processing abilities associated with learning and effective performance;
- literacy and associated skills that require more effort;
- using adequate prosody when reading;
- reading and listening comprehension (Georgiou et al., 2022);
- taking examinations, as individuals with dyslexia have inferior scores across all aspects of reading – including speed and comprehension;
- comprehension, as they need more time to understand questions (Lewandowski et al., 2016);
- calculations – in general, individuals who have specific learning disorders expend more energy and tire more rapidly when reading, writing, and making calculations (Shaywitz et al., 2016).

Other studies have shown weaknesses in:

- note taking, both in quantity and quality (Boyle, 2006, 2007; Oefinger & Peverly, 2020);
- handwriting speed (Connelly et al., 2005; Christodoulou et al., 2014);
- mental arithmetic (Callens et al., 2014);
- time estimation/dyschronia (Nicolson & Fawcett, 1995; Habib, 2021);
- everyday memory tasks, as well as executive functions such as organisation (Smith-Spark et al., 2016; Protopapa & Smith-Spark, 2022).

Providing an explanation for all of these is an essential part of promoting self-awareness and self-understanding, factors that have been shown to contribute to the success of individuals who have a learning disorder such as dyslexia (Schnieders et al., 2015). Because of the continued focus of research on literacy skills, particularly reading accuracy, as well as arguments about definition and therefore the nature of dyslexia, the difficulties listed have not been fully addressed. At present, much of the academic and popular literature does not reflect the whole picture so we only have incomplete explanations. So how do we answer the question of why the behavioural characteristics referred to exist?

Biological Differences: Genetics

Dyslexia can be acquired through brain injury, but here we are referring to developmental dyslexia, which it seems can be confidently attributed to genetic differences and resulting neurodevelopmental processes. Family and twin studies have provided evidence for 70 per cent heritability, but the latter is very complex as it is polygenic, which means that there is not a dyslexia gene but a chorus of them involved. The results of a recent large-scale international study have suggested that there are up to 42 genome-wide significant loci or fixed positions on chromosomes associated with dyslexia (Doust et al., 2022). What is inherited, however, is not a reading difficulty that is a learned skill but the genotype responsible for a particular trait, thereby affecting the development of the brain. Genes provide a blueprint for brain development and function. The phenotype is the observable expression of the information contained in a person's genetic code, including what can be observed or measured of an individual's physical, psychological, and biological make-up. Characteristics and abilities develop in response to experience and environmental factors (Karmiloff-Smith, 1994).

Genes are the product of selection, and given that in evolutionary terms reading and writing are recently developed skills, they will have no direct genetic basis, in the same way that humans have not evolved to hit a baseball or ride a horse but use evolved phylogenetic abilities. Regarding hitting a baseball, evolved abilities are those involving visual perception, depth perception, hand–eye coordination, and fine motor control, amongst others. No one would argue that we have evolved to hit baseballs with bats, but we have used other physical and cognitive abilities to enable us to do so. Reading and writing are similar: they have not evolved themselves but are based upon abilities linked to language use, information processing, and fine motor control. Reading and writing are not natural abilities; they are skills that have been invented to help us communicate and must be actively learned, ideally during childhood.

Neurological Differences

There have been considerable advances in neuroscience in recent years, and these have allowed the study of structural and functional neurological differences between people with dyslexia and those without (D'Mello & Gabrieli, 2018). The following is not intended as an exhaustive coverage but to demonstrate that simplistic perspectives on neurology, such as people with dyslexia being more right brained than left brained, are misleading and will not do. It also refutes the core-deficit hypothesis that 'pins a multiplicity of cognitive, behavioural, and neurobiological phenomena onto a single mechanistic impairment and is assumed to have the power to explain all observed profiles within a particular diagnostic category' (Astle & Fletcher-Watson, 2020, p. 432). By now we should have moved on from the classic model of the neurological basis of language production and comprehension that overemphasises the significance of the Broca and Wernicke regions of the cortex (Tremblay & Dick, 2016).

Structural Differences
Early post-mortem anatomical studies suggested that there are structural differences between the brains of people with dyslexia and those without, the latter having an asymmetrical brain, the left being larger than the right, whereas symmetry has been found amongst those with dyslexia, particularly in the planum temporale, which relates to language processing (Galaburda & Kemper, 1979). Clusters of neurones in the cortex have also been identified, reflecting altered neuronal migration (Galaburda et al., 1985). Since then, brain-imaging techniques, notably magnetic resonance imaging (MRI), have provided further information about the anatomy of the brain such as volumes of grey and white matter, the integrity of white matter, as well as the metabolites that allow for communication between cells. Scans have lent support to the neuroanatomical studies that suggest structural differences, but whole-brain analysis has shown that more than just language-based components are involved in skills such as reading. For example, differences have been found in the myelination of key brain regions that might contribute to dyslexia. Myelin is the fatty sheath that surrounds axons and helps cells conduct signals faster by increasing membrane resistance along them. Studies have focused on

the perisylvian cortex, which relates to short-term verbal memory and language processing, the conclusion being that, if dyslexia is understood in the broader context of a language disorder, these differences are not surprising (Beaulieu et al., 2020).

Functional Differences
The findings of structural studies have been supported by evidence from brain scanning. The structure and functions of the brain are closely related (McGilchrist, 2019) but are demonstrated in interactive differences, evidenced by the results of in vivo, most commonly resting-state, functional magnetic resonance imaging (fMRI). These are based on the principle that the activity of the brain is reflected in blood flow. In general, the focus has been on language-processing areas, differences being evident in several brain regions, as well as in atypical patterns of connectivity. It is not overall brain size or that of regions that correlate with general intelligence but the number and capacity of neurons. For example, although the cerebellum makes up only 10 per cent of the brain's total size, it accounts for more than 50 per cent of the total number of neurons located in the entire brain (Lee et al., 2019). Neurons talk to one another through synapses, the junctions between nerve cells that are essential for sending messages through the central nervous system. The efficiency of the brain is determined by connectivity: right to left, or the influence of the hemispheres on one another; front to back, relating to the influence of the frontal lobes on the posterior cortex; up and down, or the effects of the cortex on automatic responses in subcortical regions (Fuster, 1997; McGilchrist, 2019). Connections determine how our brain functions, and research findings have suggested that it is endogenous factors underlying successful encoding and retrieval that drive variability in performance (Kahana et al., 2018).

It goes without saying that the brain is a very complex organ and that we are a long way from understanding it fully. Imaging is useful but the results can be ambiguous, as each region of the brain is involved in a host of experiences and interacts with other regions.

Activity in some areas does not necessarily reflect higher cognitive functions that result from interactions (Satel & Lilienfeld, 2013). Nicolson and Fawcett (2019) suggest that there is a delay in the formation of the neural networks that underpin reading, and this is also reflected in the approach to studying the development of cognition known as neuroconstructivism (Broadbent & Mareschal, 2020). The latter suggests that cognition is not determined by specific independent modules as core-deficit models would imply, but rather a process that emerges over time within a dynamic system and environment. Computational modelling has been used to describe how the brain becomes more specialised. The emergence of increasingly more complex mental representations is understood to occur through processes that are dependent on experience within the context of multiple bidirectional interactions, from genome to neural networks, to the physical environment. Neuroconstructivism refers to the way in which the brain constructs cognition, representations emerging within the context of multiple interacting levels: molecular, cellular, bodily, and social events that interact and influence the establishment of cognitive representations. The conclusion is that the brain constantly changes in response to the environment. This underpins the understanding of neuroplasticity, that is, the brain's adaptability over time, which is fundamental to a developmental perspective. Neuroconstructivist principles have been applied specifically to the understanding of dyslexia (Westermann et al., 2007). It has been suggested that to understand the deficit in dyslexia, a model that integrates attention and perception, higher cognitive functions such as the representations of words in working memory and the language-specific knowledge stored in long-term memory are required (Trautmann, 2014).

There are methodological concerns about neuroscientific evidence, including small sample sizes (Ramus et al., 2018), and we are a long way from being able to identify dyslexia in individuals through fMRI scanning. We should also be avoiding the neuro-reductionism that is increasingly popular in explaining mental health conditions and neurodevelopmental disorders. This underestimates the role of developmental processes in childhood and adolescence, especially during times at which the plasticity of the brain is at its peak. Nevertheless, there is solid evidence to support the contention that there is a neurological basis related to connectivity, and neurobiological origins should not be excluded from definitions and explanations (Elliott & Grigorenko, 2024). This is contrary to those who argue that there is 'no evidence to suggest that difficulty in learning to read words accurately and fluently is associated with anything having gone wrong in brain development' (Protopapas & Parrila, 2018, p. 13). Although acknowledging that the symptoms of dyslexia are expressions of brain structure and function, they overemphasise environmental factors. Huettig et al. (2018) have gone as far as suggesting that, as a reading difficulty, dyslexia can be a secondary consequence of reduced reading experience, the latter influencing the structure and functioning of the brain, as well as processing abilities. This is a form of dualism that implies a one-way effect rather than a bidirectional process.

Because most neuroimaging studies of dyslexia have been conducted with adults who have experienced years of difficulty with reading, it has been almost impossible to determine whether the brain differences are associated with the underlying neurobiological aetiology of dyslexia or are instead the consequence of years of reduced reading experience. One of the ways of resolving this is to make comparisons based on skills such as reading at the same level. Studies match individuals who have approximately the same amount of reading experience as those with dyslexia. This approach has not been applied to adults, but in one such study, children with dyslexia, for example, exhibited reduced left-parietal and occipital-temporal activations relative to both age-matched and ability-matched children, suggesting that these hypoactivations were related to the same cause of dyslexia. Studies that matched participants based on their reading skills rather than their age showed reduced left-parietal and occipital-temporal activations amongst those who had dyslexia, implying that this is causal rather than an effect of limited reading opportunities (Norton et al., 2015).

Cognitive Differences

The study of individual differences is one of the pillars of psychology and provides a basis for understanding outcomes in domains such as cognition. It has also influenced the development of psychometric measurement and is central to theory construction (Revelle et al., 2010). Perhaps because it has been acknowledged by some that dyslexia persists across the lifespan, there has been a paradigm shift from the focus on observable behaviours to surface-level cognitive processes associated with academic skills and performance. These include phonological processing, rapid automatic naming, and working memory, which persist into adulthood and can still be identified, even amongst highly educated individuals (Moojen et al., 2020). Developments in experimental and cognitive psychology have meant that we know a great deal about the correlates of academic and work performance. There is contrary evidence and a lack of consensus, but psychology works on conceptual models. It is worth reiterating that the evidence provided by research does not necessarily demonstrate cause and effect but provides a basis for developing understanding. Theory and definitions only reflect knowledge at a particular point in time and should be refined according to current evidence, but even now we can identify cognitive weaknesses or inefficiencies that place people at risk of literacy, learning, and performance difficulties.

There is still a need for much more research into the impact on adults, particularly in employment, but we can still construct models that, even if they need refinement, enable individuals to move forward in terms of the skills and strategies they develop, as well as advocate for themselves constructively. Quantitative evidence that describes broader difficulties experienced in higher education and in the workplace is emerging, studies reporting cognitive failures in attention, prospective memory, and aspects of executive functions (see, for example, Smith-Spark et al., 2016).

There is disagreement about whether reading comprehension, not just accuracy, is also impaired in adults with dyslexia, but it has been argued that limitations in the dynamics of the brain and therefore cognition are such that inefficiencies in lower-order processes will have a bidirectional impact on higher-order functions. Consequently, fewer resources are available for the higher-level processes involved in text comprehension, readers having to use strategies to achieve adequate comprehension levels. These include slow and effortful reading, making use of general verbal ability, as well as exploring text structure to help process the content. A similar argument can be made to address the matter of why people with dyslexia seem to experience difficulties with executive functions such as planning, time estimation, and organisation. There is, however, evidence to support the notion that some of these might be intrinsic to dyslexia (Brosnan et al., 2002; Leather et al., 2011; Smith-Spark et al., 2016).

Non-cognitive Attributes

In the post-Covid era, the mental health of children, adolescents, and adults has been of concern, and it is important to acknowledge that learning disorders can relate to it. Neurodevelopmental disorders 'can significantly impact a person's mental health and overall functioning. Conversely mental health conditions such as anxiety and depression can also arise from or in conjunction with neurodevelopmental disorders' (Papadopoulos, 2023, p. 4). Over the past 20 years or more, systematic studies have provided objective evidence that demonstrates the impact learning disorders can have on emotional development in adulthood (Nalavany et al., 2011). Historically, they have been referred to as secondary characteristics, resulting from the experience of having dyslexia, but the preferred term is now non-cognitive attributes. These are not caused by having dyslexia, but as with information problems they put people at risk (Gregg, 2014). Studies involving undergraduates have demonstrated that persisting difficulties in reading and writing as well as studying generally can contribute to anxiety, low self-esteem, and lack of confidence (Abbott-

Jones, 2021; Brunswick & Bargary, 2022). Adolescents and adults with dyslexia can experience more adaptation difficulties than others, especially because of the effort required to meet increased demands, including those that need high levels of literacy. The requirement to make greater effort to meet academic and performance levels can lead to frustration and anxiety when people are faced with tasks that prove challenging. These individuals often require more family support as well as professional help throughout their education and careers (Carawan et al., 2016), and exhibit more depressive symptoms than their peers without dyslexia (Moojen et al., 2020).

DYSLEXIA AS A DISABILITY

Classifications such as ICD-11 no longer use categories including dyslexia, instead referring to disorders in reading, a disorder being a description of symptoms, behaviours, and actions of a person characterised by an impairment and a disruption to usual functioning. If dyslexia is genetic in origin, is neurologically based, and has an impact on day-to-day activities, it can be perceived as a disorder. Dyslexia comes under the heading of developmental learning disorder: an impairment that is characterised by significant and persisting difficulties in learning academic skills related to reading such as word-reading accuracy, reading fluency, and reading comprehension. The individual's performance in reading is markedly below what would be expected for chronological age and level of intellectual functioning, resulting in a significant impairment in the person's academic or occupational functioning. Exclusionary criteria include it not being due to low intelligence, sensory impairment, neurological disorder, poor education, or lack of proficiency in the language of instruction.

Dyslexia can be considered a disability under the terms of the United Kingdom Equality Act 2010 and the Americans with Disabilities Act of 1990. In the former a disability is described as 'a physical or mental impairment that has a substantial effect on day-to-day activities' (Equality Act 2010, s. 6). *Cognitive* would be preferable to *mental*, but the key words are 'impairment', 'substantial', and 'day-to-day'. When disputes arise between employers and employees resulting in a tribunal matter, the first question is whether these criteria are met. The range of people with dyslexia will include those for whom it does not have a substantial impact on their day-to-day lives. Both 'substantial' and 'day-to-day' are contextual. Being a slow reader might not be of significance much of the time, but for people who must take examinations for promotion, for example, it might become so.

There have essentially been two models of disability: the social model that attributes the problems experienced by people to society, and the medical model that views disability as a feature of the individual that requires treatment. This dichotomy has been the subject of much debate, and some advocates for the social model have changed their mind, acknowledging that both individual and societal factors must be considered (Shakespeare, 2013). The medical model has had considerable criticism, including the suggestion that it promotes normalisation through treatment, which is harmful to those who have disabilities (Zaks, 2024). It has been suggested that the social model creates an 'us and them' mentality (Runswick-Cole, 2014) and fosters a sense of grievance that suits the more strident amongst advocacy movements but does little to help promote understanding and empathy. Developmental disorders are neither medical nor social. Research into factors that contribute to the success of people who have learning disabilities has acknowledged that it is a result of both the internal and the external (Gerber et al., 1992). The answer to this polarisation lies in acknowledging the biopsychosocial model (Harris & McDade, 2018; Doyle, 2020) by integrating the biological, the psychological, and the social. At the psychological level the emphasis regarding neurodevelopmental disorders should be on cognition, as well as the interaction between processing abilities and social factors.

Over the years individuals who have neurodevelopmental disorders have variously been described as atypical, exceptional, and extraordinary. Increasingly, there is reference to the neurodiverse, and the use of terminology such as neurominority (Milton, 2019). When new language and terminology is introduced, the question to be answered is whether it will lead to improvements in understanding, whether this be an individual's self-understanding or that of others in educational and workplace settings; otherwise it is too easily adopted without clearly thinking through the implications. The term neurodiversity originated amongst the more articulate within the autism advocacy movement in the United States, and much of the literature addressing the concept focuses on autism. It belongs to the social model of disability, although there has been debate amongst activists as to whether it should be applied to all individuals on the autistic spectrum or just those who are considered to be 'high functioning', the latter not being representative of the autistic population as a whole. It has been adopted, often inappropriately, by professionals working with, and groups advocating for, those who have neurodevelopmental disorders such as dyslexia, and the same issue arises. Accomplished adults with dyslexia might prefer to be thought of as different rather than disabled, but those who are functionally illiterate and face daily humiliation, having to rely on others to deal with the most basic of literacy tasks, are unlikely to see themselves as being neurodiverse. In a world in which written communication has become increasingly important, the latter can constantly feel judged by others because they cannot read and write.

The term neurodiversity is ill-defined, being used both adjectivally and nominatively. It adds nothing to understanding underlying difficulties; it simply indicates membership of a group. The muddle surrounding it is perhaps best characterised by the title of a paper: 'The myth of the normal brain: Embracing neurodiversity' (Armstrong, 2015). If the idea of a so-called normal brain is a myth, why do we need to talk about diverse brains? One can only define neurotypicality by exclusion. That is, if someone is not neurodiverse, they are neurotypical.

Until the concept has been clearly defined, beyond its use as a slogan, it is unhelpful, particularly regarding syndromes such as dyslexia for which there is a strong evidence base. It does nothing to contribute to understanding, either self-understanding or that of others, preventing people from developing the most important skill they can have, which is knowing how to advocate for themselves. It is not a diagnosis, nor does it reflect a paradigm shift as it has been recognised for many years that people learn, think, and work differently, thus the *psychology of individual differences*. It is why not everyone is a labourer, a lawyer, a doctor, an engineer, an artist, or an architect. The episteme on which neurodiversity is based is flawed, its proponents fitting research findings to theory, thus engaging in concept-based evidence making, and it is anti-scientific. Neurodiversity is a euphemism that belongs to the politics of advocacy, celebrating a neurobiological identity that overlooks the importance of developmental processes throughout the lifespan, as well as the interaction between biological and environmental factors (Anastasiou, 2024). It is not surprising that it appeals to the advocacy movement, particularly self-advocacy groups, and it might have increased social acceptance and fostered a more inclusive environment in education and employment, as well as helped individuals develop a positive self-identity. Nevertheless, it does not belong to scientific enquiry, nor the evidence-based practice of psychology. Kauffman (2007) wrote that 'when we believe that people should be allowed to make up realities to suit their situations, regardless of the facts, we are courting practical, moral, professional, and political disasters' (p. 245).

Having dyslexia can be the most disabling when individuals do not understand themselves, they are not understood by others, do not have the opportunity to develop the skills they need, adjustments are not made for them, and they cannot advocate for themselves constructively. Regarding the last point, people should not indulge in celebrating their neurobiological identity, defining themselves through their disability. Provided they have the necessary skills, abilities, and competencies, no one should be prevented from pursuing an educational programme or career, particularly if they have found ways of mitigating the impact of dyslexia on their performance. Only identifying themselves in terms of their disability will not lead to them being better understood and can lead to the lowering of expectations. It is for this reason that we refer here to *people with dyslexia*. They are people first and foremost.

THE WAY FORWARD

At present we have partial explanations for parts of a problem. We need to bring together the data from research so that we can develop clear explanations and definitions if people are to understand themselves and they are to be understood by others. It is no surprise to learn that employees who have a disability complain that they feel discriminated against despite the existence of legislation to prevent this (Deacon et al., 2022; Olsen, 2024). If they do not understand themselves and their needs, they will not be able to explain their specific difficulties and suggest solutions. This is not to say that the emphasis and responsibility end with the person who has dyslexia, but they need to be able to advocate for themselves based upon their self-understanding and individual differences. Without that, they fall victim to the negative stereotypes held by the uninformed and the poorly informed. Being different should not prevent people from succeeding in life, but to just focus on that can raise expectations and lead to failure.

We should not, however, just focus on why people with dyslexia find tasks difficult. There are empirical studies that have considered the factors that enable individuals who have learning disorders to succeed (Schnieders et al., 2015). These are described in Chapter 9 as they are important to career guidance and development, as well as the ways in which individuals can be supported in education and in the workplace. Suffice it to say at this point that self-understanding is paramount.

Philosopher of science Lipton (2017) wrote that 'Understanding is not some sort of super knowledge, but simply more knowledge:

knowledge of causes' (p. 30). What is required is a theoretical explanatory model derived from empirical data that can incorporate and integrate the various findings of systematic research to provide *the likeliest explanation*, that is, the one most warranted by the data. From that, through inference, we can work towards '*the loveliest explanation* which, if correct, provides the most understanding' (Lipton, 2017, p. 207, our emphasis).

Based on existing literature, our own data, and practical experience, we argue here that inefficient working-memory ability is a cognitive marker of dyslexia. This is not a new idea, as can be seen from the research cited in this chapter, and we have adopted it throughout the time we have worked with adults with dyslexia (McLoughlin et al., 1994; McLoughlin & Leather, 2013). We are proposing here that a cohesive working-memory model provides one of the loveliest explanations as it:

- can account for difficulties beyond reading;
- predict future challenges;
- provide a rationale for strategy development.

In Chapter 3 we provide an analysis of a large dataset that describes persisting behavioural difficulties experienced by people with dyslexia, as well as cognitive weaknesses that might explain these.

SUMMARY

The main points of this chapter, in which we have focused on the evidence for dyslexia as a learning disorder, include:

- discussing the various definitions and diagnostic criteria for dyslexia;
- placing dyslexia in the context of a lifespan perspective;
- promoting the PSW model for definition and diagnosis;
- outlining the behavioural characteristics reported in research literature;
- describing the findings of research at a biological level, both from genetics and neuroscience, as well as the cognitive and non-cognitive characteristics that derive from these;
- considering different perspectives on disorders and disability.

3 Evidence from Practice

INTRODUCTION

There are many influences on the reasons why scientists and practitioners adopt particular models for their research and clinical work. Our interest in information processing is based on our experience as scientist practitioners who conduct individual assessments, relying on measures of cognitive abilities to explain inconsistencies in an individual's performance. It is reinforced by the scientific literature, systematic studies having considered dyslexia within the context of information processing, including its involvement in academic skills and everyday functioning (see, for example, McLoughlin & Leather, 2013).

Here we present an analysis of archive data based on the results of 1,423 differential cognitive and literacy assessments conducted over a 10-year period that show that processing weaknesses are a persistent issue for adults experiencing problems with literacy, learning, life, and employment-related skills. The data demonstrates a consistent pattern of low working ability and variation within it in all cognitive ability domains. The analysis has implications for the appropriate assessment of dyslexia, as well as interventions, especially as it persists across the lifespan.

In a sense there should be no such thing as a dyslexia test, nor a dyslexia assessor. There are many reasons why someone might find the development of skills such as literacy, numeracy, and learning generally challenging, and an assessment should identify the most salient factors. Establishing that someone has dyslexia should not just be a labelling exercise, but one of explanation. It is a process known as differential diagnosis, which should do the following:

- Show what people can and might be able to do. This is why abilities such as verbal and non-verbal reasoning, vocabulary, and spatial ability are measured. These can also be helpful in assisting people to achieve the 'goodness of fit' important to success (see Chapter 9).
- Measure performance in academic skills such as literacy, as well as processing abilities associated with those, so inconsistencies can be considered.
- Provide an explanation for inconsistencies that promotes the most understanding, self-understanding, and understanding by others.
- Provide a rationale for solutions so individuals can engage in deliberate strategy development.

Too often people have been given a label but not an explanation for their difficulties, so they are unable to become proactive in seeking solutions and advocate for themselves. This can be the result of a tick box, or checklist, approach. We do not want to explore a binary versus spectrum approach; however, a meaningful measured cognitive evaluation respects the fact that differences in abilities can result in problems with functions.

It is not unusual to meet people who were tested at school, provided with learning support, and allowed extra time in examinations but still do not know why or how to use that extra time. The individuals sometimes say they and/or their family were told they have slow processing speed, but it is often clear that they do not understand what this means. Even more problematically, some see this as a euphemism for a lack of *general* ability, a rationale for them being labelled as 'slow' or 'stupid', rather than a *specific* difficulty with aspects of processing.

Sometimes it is as obvious that the person conducting the assessment does not know why they are administering specific tests. Unfortunately, the diagnostic process has too often become a bureaucratic exercise in accessing resources and accommodations, whereas Shaywitz et al. (2016) have written that 'self-awareness and self-knowledge, gained by an accurate diagnosis of dyslexia, bring in the light and allow the person to understand himself, to know how he functions and learns, the nature of his difficulties, and how to help himself' (p. 283).

ASSESSMENT PROTOCOL

The testing reported here was conducted by the same educational psychologist, relying on a protocol developed over time in response to recognising the nature of dyslexia as it presents itself amongst accomplished adults, as well as the literature relating to the identification of dyslexia during the adult years. We adopt a parsimonious approach, particularly as the older individuals become, the less likely they are to want to undergo exhaustive testing. Some clients report having had previous assessments that lasted multiple hours, which they recall with some residual trauma. The approach described here consists of an interview focusing on matters such as health, educational and occupational background, as well as perceived difficulties, and then the administration of the following tests.

Cognitive and Processing Abilities

- The Wechsler Adult Intelligence Scale, 4th edition (WAIS-IV) (Wechsler, 2008);
- Measures of rapid-naming ability from the Comprehensive Test of Phonological Processing (CTOPP) (Wagner et al., 1999).

Literacy

- Prose-reading and silent-reading comprehension passages from the Spadafore Diagnostic Reading Test (SDRT) (Spadafore, 1983);
- The spelling scale from the Wechsler Individual Achievement Test, 3rd edition (WIAT-III) (Wechsler, 2017);
- The writing and proofreading scales from the York Adult Assessment Battery-Revised (YAA-R) (Warmington et al., 2012);
- The sight word-reading scale from the Test of Word Reading Efficiency (TOWRE) (Torgesen et al., 1999).

The results for the cognitive and processing tests are expressed as standard scores using the standard IQ scale where the population mean is 100 and the standard deviation is 15 points. Percentiles are included to aid interpretation. Based upon this, it is assumed that just over two thirds of the population should have an IQ score between 85 and 115 points (one standard deviation either side of the mean), and around 95 per cent of the population should score between 70 and 130 (two standard deviations).

In assessing literacy, the view taken here is that 'we need the skills we need', so essentially the results are criterion referenced. Tests of reading accuracy that yield comparative scores are inadequate. Reading skills are rated here as being at one of four levels, professional being the highest (defined in the SDRT, 1983). Writing speed is expressed as words per minute, and proofreading as a percentage of errors identified. Spelling skills are evaluated qualitatively, the best judge of competence in spelling during the adult years being able to use electronic devices.

The criteria for diagnosis used here are adapted from ICD-11 as it considers comparisons with a person's own intellectual abilities, not just the average for a population, and extends beyond reading accuracy to skills such as reading fluency and comprehension. Separate criteria are used for difficulties in writing and spelling. As suggested in Chapters 1 and 2, we are considering unexpected areas of underperformance but also going beyond these and providing evidence of processing weaknesses that might explain them.

COGNITIVE ABILITIES

There are several comprehensive tests in common use, but internationally and over nearly seven decades in the field of learning disorders, the Wechsler Adult Intelligence Scales (WAIS) have been the most widely used. They are also used in a variety of settings, including neuropsychology, and can be interpreted at multiple levels:

- global composite: full-scale IQ;
- specific composite: index scores;
- subtest level;
- item level;
- task cognitive capacities.

This means the WAIS can be used as a normative test, allowing comparison with others of the same age, and an ipsative test, allowing for examination of contrasts between an individual's own abilities. As a diagnostic instrument, it is at its best when used as an ipsative test.

WAIS-IV as a Normative Test

The WAIS-IV consists of 15 subtests that tap different abilities: four verbal, five perceptual reasoning, three working memory, and three processing speed. It provides a full-scale IQ and four index scores, the latter being based on core subtests. The subtests and the abilities they purport to measure are described later in this chapter, but it should be noted that although the subtests are designed to measure specific abilities, it is a mistake to assume that they are 'pure', as they each necessarily involve several, sometimes overlapping, processes (e.g. verbal comprehension of instructions).

The Global Composite: Full-Scale IQ

Although designed as a measure of intelligence originally defined by Wechsler as the 'capacity of the individual to act purposefully, to think rationally, and to deal effectively with his environment' (Wechsler et al., 2008, p. 3), in the context of identifying a syndrome such as dyslexia, the full-scale IQ of WAIS-IV is its least useful measure. It will distinguish between the less able and those who have specific difficulties, but because some of the subtests tap the areas of cognitive weakness associated with dyslexia, the full-scale score can result in an underestimate of intellectual potential. People with dyslexia can find some of the subtests more difficult than others, primarily the working-memory and processing-speed tests, so a full-scale IQ will give the impression of an artificially lower overall ability. In general, and whatever the test used, calculation of a global IQ score when working with individuals who have a specific learning disorder should be discouraged. It is variability that characterises the adaptability implicit in Wechsler's definition.

The Specific Composite: Index Scores

As well as a full-scale IQ score, the WAIS-IV allows for the calculation of four index scores: verbal comprehension, perceptual reasoning, working memory, and processing speed. Figure 3.1 summarises the structure of the WAIS-IV, showing each of the index scales along with its associated core subtests. Each of the index scales also has at least one supplemental (optional) subtest (shown in italics), which can be administered in addition or as an alternative to the core subtests.

The index scores provide useful diagnostic information, the discrepancies between them being regarded as a broad but often useful guide to evidence of a learning disorder. They also provide measures of competencies, and this enables an assessor to inform clients of what they can do, as well as explain why some things are difficult for them. Identifying abilities, notably language skills such as vocabulary, verbal reasoning, and comprehension, is important as they underlie the development of reading skills. Without an adequate vocabulary, for example, skills such as reading comprehension will be impaired (Swanson, 2015). Information about competencies is helpful in

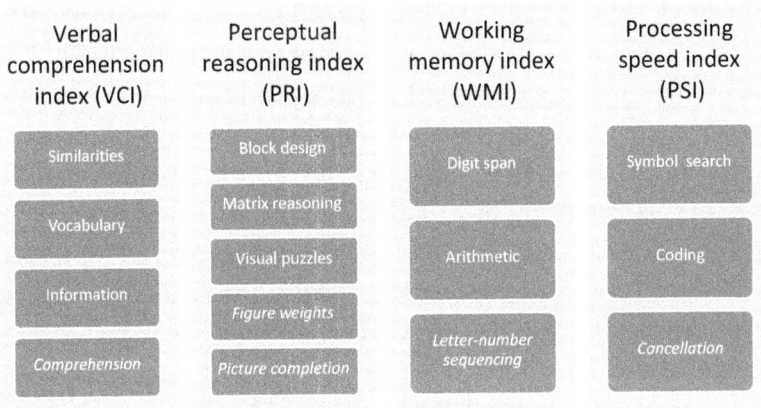

FIGURE 3.1 The structure of the WAIS-IV assessment showing indices and associated subtests.

providing academic and career guidance. For example, individuals who have an average or better-than-average perceptual reasoning index score are likely to be more suited to occupations involving visual perceptual skills. Abilities such as verbal comprehension have been identified as good predictors of success at university and in making the transition from school to employment. This is elaborated upon in Chapter 9 of this book.

The Subtest Level: WAIS-IV as an Ipsative Test

The WAIS-IV measures a wide range of abilities, and people with dyslexia often show an uneven profile, reflecting contrasting strengths and weaknesses. Ipsative testing refers to consideration of the potential implications of such contrasts within an individual's profile. Over the years a considerable amount of research has been devoted to identifying 'typical' dyslexic profiles of Wechsler subtest scores. This can be a somewhat forlorn endeavour in our view because of the variation within the category of people labelled 'dyslexic'. It is far better to assess the person using the ability measures, skills assessment, and their own self-report than to fit them to a 'type'.

The *Technical and interpretive manual for WAIS-IV* (Wechsler, 2010) lists a range of specialist group studies. In this context those most likely to be of interest are those described as individuals with learning disorders, including reading disorders (dyslexia), mathematics disorders (dyscalculia), as well as attentional disorders (ADD/ADHD). Classification of the disorders in the WAIS-IV is based on the *Diagnostic and statistical manual of mental disorders, fourth edition, text revision* (DSM-IV-TR) (American Psychiatric Association, 2000) criteria and, therefore, on a discrepancy model, and the studies are small in terms of their sample size and for limited age groups. Nevertheless, it is worth noting that, in general, individuals with reading disorders (dyslexia) scored lower on the working-memory index than on the other indices, lending support to the argument opposing the calculation of a full-scale IQ.

The Item Level and Developed Strategies

The greater emphasis on information processing in WAIS-IV is reflected in the provision of *component scores*. For example, there are three component parts to the digit span subtest. They are designed to facilitate the qualitative analysis many psychologists already conduct by providing objective scores for the cognitive abilities that can contribute to subtest performance. They are not, however, a substitute for a subtest score or used in the calculation of index scores.

In the test manual for WAIS-IV, the authors have made recommendations regarding the use of supplemental tests in the calculation of a composite score. They have suggested that this be done when the subtest performance is invalidated by factors such as administration errors, recent exposure to test items, and response sets. This is an important consideration when assessing individuals who have a neurodevelopmental disorder. One might, for example, use Cancellation rather than Coding when problems with fine motor skills are evident as it does not require the formation of symbols. Further, it is not unusual for adults to have developed strategies that enable them to deal with working-memory tasks, for example, 'chunking' when remembering series of numbers and relying on their fingers to help with mental calculations. These might be regarded as invalidating factors, the intention being to measure ability rather than strategy use. In general, it becomes increasingly difficult to distinguish between ability and strategy as people mature and rely on the expertise they have acquired. In addition, anxiety can be an additional factor that masks potential ability. The present authors, for example, prefer letter-number sequencing to arithmetic as the former is less influenced by experience, including the humiliation some people have suffered in the past when it has been obvious to others that mental arithmetic has been a problem for them.

RESULTS

The Sample

Those in this client sample were referred for testing by either their educational institution or their employer, or they were self-referred.

The assessments were all based upon assumptions that the individuals might have dyslexia, but they might have also raised other co-morbid difficulties, the most commonly reported of which being dyspraxia, dyscalculia, ADHD, or ADD.

Broadly, there is almost always one of two types of individuals: those in education or those in employment. Education referrals usually involved those studying in higher education (university) and sometimes within further education (vocational and access courses). Employment referrals were usually the result of perceived shortcomings in performance recognised by the employee or employer. The more recent trend towards apprenticeship courses for people in employment but in part assessed by university providers are not represented here. The sample does, however, include those studying for professional qualifications and specialist postgraduate training in occupations such as medicine and law.

All 1,423 assessments reported here were conducted over a 10-year period. Male participants within the sample were more likely to be referred for employment purposes (62.0 per cent) than education (38.0 per cent). Female participants were only slightly more likely to be referred for employment purposes (53.5 per cent) than education (46.5 per cent). The age of the sample ranges from 18 to 78, the mean being 29.4 years (standard deviation of 11.6 years) with a larger proportion of younger adults represented, so the age range is positively skewed. There were 707 females (mean age 29.1 years) and 716 males (mean age of 29.7 years). Of these, 601 were university students (mean age 21.7) and 822 were employed in a range of occupations (mean age 35.1) seeking assessments for the workplace.

Cognitive Abilities

The Wechsler intelligence scales have been the most widely used measure of cognitive abilities in the field of learning disorders. There are three versions: one for testing preschool children between the ages of four and six years (Wechsler Preschool and Primary Scale of Intelligence – WPPSI), one for testing children between the ages of 6 and 16 years (Wechsler Intelligence Scale for Children – WISC), and one for adolescents and adults from 16 to 90 years old (WAIS). They have each been revised on a regular basis, about every 15 years or so. Each revision provides the current norms and is redesigned to reflect advances in theoretical and practical foundations of cognitive ability and neuropsychological assessment (Zhu & Weiss, 2005). The latest version of the adult scales (WAIS-IV) is, therefore, based on clinical research and theoretical development. WAIS-V, the next version yet to be published in the United Kingdom but available in the United States at the time of writing (early 2025) (Wechsler, 2024), reflects the way in which the scales develop as it includes new measures of processing abilities. The test battery is effectively the collective name for a set of subtests that are designed to measure different aspects of cognitive ability. These reflect a dynamic relationship amongst processing speed, working memory, reasoning, and learning. The Wechsler scales are a set of very-well-established cognitive neurological assessments: cognitive because they are designed to assess abilities such as a person's understanding and information processing, and neurological because these cognitive abilities are known to be linked to specific functionality in the brain.

The Wechsler Intelligence Scales break these cognitive abilities down into four domains referred to as indices (and reported as index scores). These are the product of two binary-type categorisations. The first binary type of assessment is verbal and non-verbal ability (which in the WAIS assessments was historically called performance ability). This distinction between verbal and non-verbal ability is found throughout the cognitive ability assessment literature. The second binary type of assessment is understanding and information processing. This division between understanding, sometimes referred to as concrete ability, and information processing, sometimes referred to as fluid ability, is also found throughout the cognitive ability assessment literature (Lezak et al., 2012). As shown in Figure 3.2, this combination of verbal and non-verbal ability with understanding and information-processing ability results in four distinct categories. The

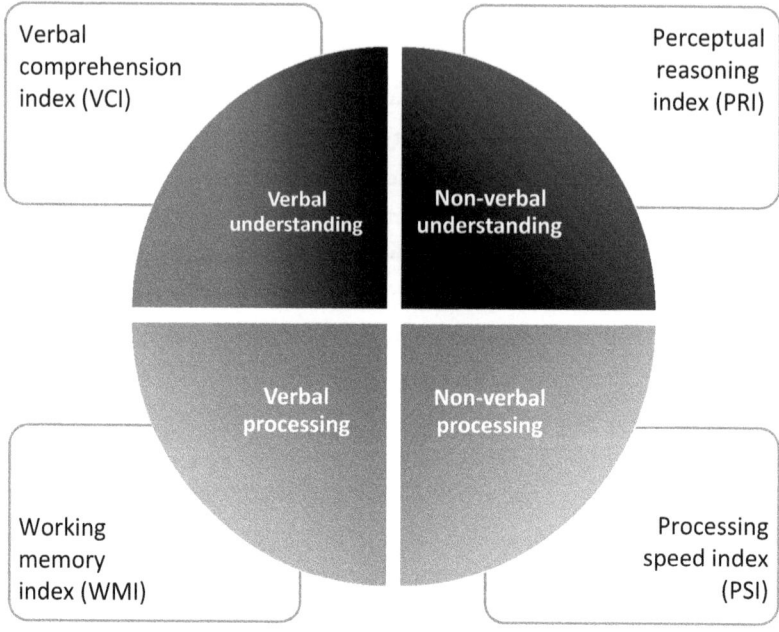

FIGURE 3.2 WAIS-IV conceptual structure.

measurement of these within the WAIS-IV are the index scales, each of which has a specific name presented in Figure 3.2.

As already noted, the WAIS-IV includes indices for verbal comprehension (VCI), perceptual reasoning (PRI), working memory (WMI), and processing speed (PSI). These indices are based on a two-by-two construct design involving verbal and non-verbal ability in one construct, and knowledge and processing in the other.

Figure 3.2 shows that working memory is one of the four index scales. The focus here is not on working-memory management alone because it must be considered in the context of the other ability measurements. An elaboration of what each of these index scales is purporting to measure as well as the multiple subtests that go together to make up each of the index scales follows. The aim of this is to provide a better understanding of working memory within the context of other cognitive abilities, and a little more about the way in

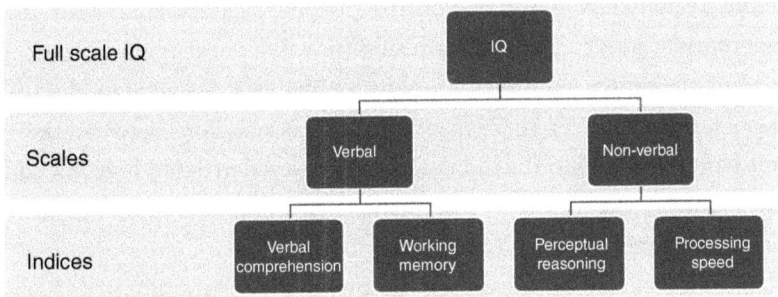

FIGURE 3.3 WAIS-IV hierarchical structure.

which it is measured using psychological assessment tools such as the Weschler Intelligence Scales (adult and child).

In this section each of the index scales is outlined and a general description of what the subtests are supposed to measure is provided. The formal names of each of the subtests are within parentheses when referred to in the text. This description is not intended to be a thorough and technical account of each of the index scales and subtests, but to assist in understanding what each of the measures is designed to assess so that the data presented here can be interpreted appropriately. The hierarchical structure of the WAIS-IV is shown in Figure 3.3. This should help remind us of where each index is located in relation to the verbal and non-verbal scales and the full-scale IQ.

Most of the subtests within each of the index scales become more difficult as the test proceeds. The exceptions to this are the two processing-speed index subtests (Coding and Symbol search), which are measures of how many elements of the subtest the respondent can complete within the time limit. All the subtests, again except the processing-speed index ones, have a discontinue rule that consists of a specific number of consecutive incorrect responses that result in the subtest being discontinued early; otherwise, the assessor will administer all the subtest items.

The test is hierarchically structured, as depicted in Figure 3.3, such that each of the subtests assesses a distinct cognitive ability, or more realistically a set of abilities, which is associated with the appropriate index. The test batteries are validated using a statistical technique known as confirmatory factor analysis, designed to identify associations between these measures. The associations between these measures and within the indices are not covered in detail here but can be found in the WAIS-IV test manual and other publicly available texts (see Lichtenberger & Kaufman, 2012).

The reason for presenting the hierarchical structure is to highlight that, typically, the scores on the WAIS-IV will be strongly associated (technically, correlated) within any group of respondents. What this means is that within any sample of people assessed using the WAIS-IV, those who score the highest on any subtest or index will also tend to score highest on the other subtests and indices, and vice versa for those who score the lowest (the subtests and indices tend to be positively correlated). This also means that when we plot a person's individual scores on the four indices or the subtests that they have completed, they will typically score at a similar level on all the measures. However, if a specific index or subtest is lower than expected, it could be indicative of an underlying problem. For example, in identifying dyslexia within an adult population using the WAIS-IV, the working-memory index, or at least one of its composite subtests, will tend to be lower than the other cognitive indices (Wechsler, 2008).

The *verbal comprehension index* (VCI) scale consists of a group of tests designed to assess a person's *verbal understanding*. The subtests focus on a person's understanding of word meanings (Vocabulary), verbal concepts (Similarities), and their general knowledge of information communicated verbally (Information). None of these subtests require the respondent to read any information. The respondent need only provide verbal explanations of their understanding and does not have to, in fact is not permitted to, write down any information. In addition, none of these tests are time limited.

The *perceptual reasoning index* (PRI) scale consists of a group of tests designed to assess a person's *non-verbal understanding*. The subtests focus on a person's understanding of underlying visual patterns (Matrix reasoning), the replication of visual patterns using physical blocks (Block design), and their ability to carry out visuo-spatial reasoning (Visual puzzles). All these subtests require that the respondent sees and perceives visual stimuli presented to them within a physical assessment booklet. One of the subtests requires that the person completing the test physically manipulate a set of plastic blocks to recreate a pattern they can see within the test booklet (Block design); the other subtests only require a verbal response. Two of the subtests are time limited (Block design and Visual puzzles), and one of these also has variable points scored based upon how quickly the person completes the subtest (Block design). The other subtest has no timed element or time limit (Matrix reasoning).

The *working-memory index* (WMI) scale consists of a group of tests designed to assess a person's *verbal information processing*. The subtests focus on the person's ability to rote recall a set of digits presented to them verbally (Digit span) and to carry out mental arithmetic (Arithmetic). For both subtests the information that has to be processed is presented by the assessor verbally, hence their inclusion in the verbal index of information processing. One of the subtests has a time limit for the respondent's answer (Arithmetic); for the other subtest, the longer the person takes to respond the less likely they are to rote recall the digits – however, there is no specific time limit. The Digit span subtest has three components: forwards, backwards, and sequencing. The Digit span forwards (DSF) requires that the respondent repeat a series of digits they have heard in the same order as presented. This measures short-term memory, but also attention and auditory processing. The Digit span reversed (DSR) requires that the respondent repeat a series of digits they have heard in reverse order (backwards). This is regarded as one of the best measures of working memory because it involves the necessary retention and manipulation of information in working memory. Digit span sequencing (DSS) requires that the respondent recite the digits they have heard in sequence from numerically lowest to highest, and this also taps into working-memory functioning. The overall index score for working memory does not, therefore, tell the whole story.

In most of the assessments referred to soon, the supplementary subtest Letter-number sequencing (LNS) has been administered rather than arithmetic. Letter-number sequencing requires that the respondent reorder a sequence containing both letters and digits. This has been described as a good measure of working memory (Crowe, 2000), involving information processing and cognitive flexibility (Lichtenberger & Kaufman, 2012). Letter-number sequencing is less prone to influence by negative educational experiences associated with mental arithmetic than the arithmetic subtest outlined earlier; because of this, it was the preferred subtest used in assessing working memory.

The *processing-speed index* (PSI) scale consists of two tests designed to assess a person's *non-verbal information processing*. The subtests focus on an individual's ability to enter coded symbols into a grid quickly (Coding) and to identify matching pairs of symbols within a short series (Symbol search). Both subtests require that the respondent use a pen or pencil to record their responses in an answer booklet. They are, therefore, the only subtests that require any 'written' response, but the responses do not involve writing any text. Both tests have a time limit of two minutes, during which the respondent must complete as many items as possible. Processing speed is often portrayed as a single ability, but it has been subdivided into four underlying factors: complex, memory, pattern recognition, and scanning ability. The memory aspect, which represents incidental memory and associated learning, is highly correlated with working memory (Ackerman et al., 2002).

In many diagnostic assessment reports where a trained psychologist is presenting data to support the case that a person has dyslexia, there is a tendency to focus on the relative deficits within the profile and specifically the deficits in the working-memory domain. However, it is important to highlight that the WAIS-IV assessment enables us to understand both strengths and weaknesses within the respondent's cognitive abilities. To help respondents make optimal decisions about current and future careers, education, and training, it is as important to understand their strengths as it is to focus on their relative weaknesses. People with dyslexia, especially those receiving a late diagnosis, have often experienced repeated, explicit reminders of their limitations during their education and in the workplace. What they need is practical advice about how they can work around these difficulties using different strategies and technology that fit the cognitive profile and align with their aims and objectives in a realistic way.

DATA ANALYSIS

Subtest Scores

Figure 3.4 shows the client sample mean scores on each of the WAIS-IV subtests (the error bars represent the 95 per cent confidence interval (CI) range). Along the x-axis (horizontal) are the WAIS-IV subtests ordered by the associated indices. The first three are the subtests of the verbal comprehension index (VCI): Similarities (S), Vocabulary (V), and Information (I). The next three are the subtests of the perceptual

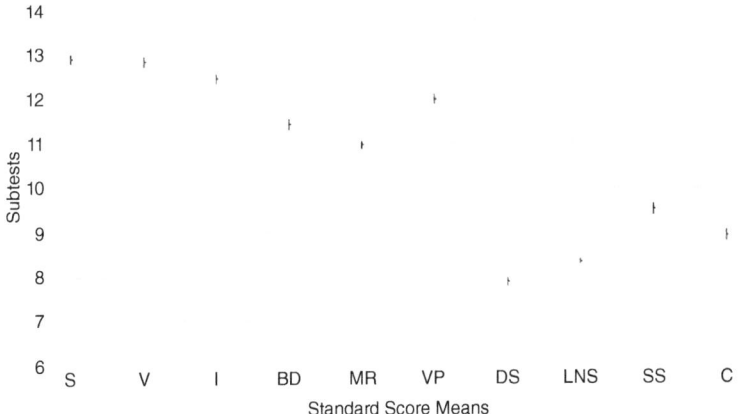

FIGURE 3.4 Sample mean scores of the WAIS-IV subtests (with 95 per cent CI).

reasoning index (PRI): Block design (BD), Matrix reasoning (MR), and Visual puzzles (VP). Next are the two working-memory index (WMI) subtests: Digit span (DS) and Letter-number sequencing (LNS). Finally, there are the processing-speed index (PSI) subtests: Symbol search (SS) and Coding (C).

The y-axis (vertical) shows the mean scores for the subtests of the WAIS-IV. The subtests use standard score parameters (they are all converted to the same range of scores). The average score for the population is 10, and the standard deviation, a measure of variation from the mean, is 3. These scores are normally distributed (bell curve shaped) in the population, and so we expect that just over two thirds of the population (68 per cent) score within one standard deviation either side of the mean (so between 7 and 13 on this scale).

Figure 3.4 shows that the three verbal comprehension index (VCI) subtest scores are the highest within the sample. The Similarities (S) and Vocabulary (V) subtests have the highest mean scores, and a great deal of overlap between their CI ranges means they are not likely to be significantly different. The Information (I) subtest is somewhat lower but still higher than all the other non-verbal comprehension index subtest scores.

These demonstrate that the client sample's strongest abilities are in the verbal understanding domain (verbal comprehension in the WAIS). The mean scores for this sample are around one standard deviation above the expected population score, indicating that the sample's mean score is in about the 80th percentile (the top 20 per cent of the population).

The next highest subtest scores are for the three PRI scores: Visual puzzles (VP), Block design (BD), and Matrix reasoning (MR). These subtests all assess aspects of non-verbal understanding. It may be noteworthy that the two timed subtests, VP and BD, are the highest scoring of the three. MR is a measure of abstract reasoning and is the lowest scoring of the three perceptual reasoning subtests. The mean scores for these subtests are all above the population mean score (10).

Some distance below the perceptual reasoning measures are the two processing-speed subtests: Symbol search (SS) and Coding (C). The tests are the only ones that require the respondent to use a pen in their completion. Both symbol search and coding are timed, and the respondent needs to work quickly under time pressure. The tasks both require visual scanning and psychomotor speed. The mean scores for these subtests are all below the population mean score (10).

Finally, the lowest two subtests are from the working-memory index: Letter-number sequencing (LNS) and Digit span (DS). These both require aspects of working memory with basic rote recall and some information retention and processing. These are the lowest subtest scores in the sample.

Note that the CIs (95 per cent) are quite narrow for these scores. This is because the sample size is so large, and the CI is based upon the standard error of the standard deviation.

Figure 3.5 includes the means and standard deviations for each of the measures. Given the sample sizes, we can assume these are good estimates for these groups. The difference from Figure 3.4 is that the standard deviation is not adjusted for by sample size (called the

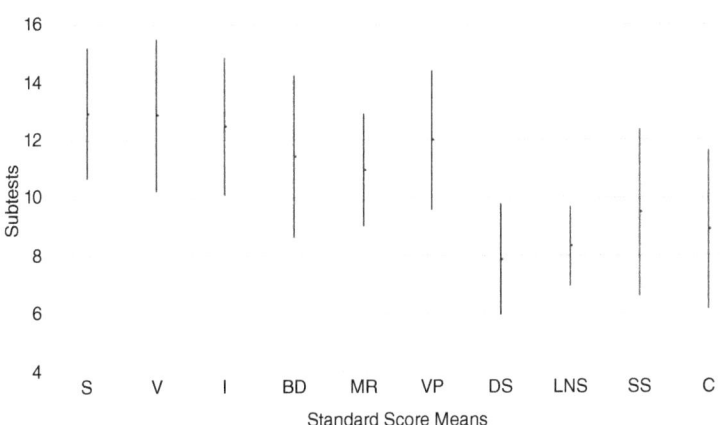

FIGURE 3.5 Sample mean scores of the WAIS-IV subtests (with standard deviation error bars).

standard error, presented in Figure 3.5). This gives us an accurate estimate of the true spread of the scores within the population.

It should be noted that the mean scores are, of course, the same as those presented in Figure 3.4. However, here we can see that one standard deviation below the mean for all the verbal ability measures (Similarities, Vocabulary, and Information) is higher than the one standard deviation above the mean for the two working-memory measures (Digit span and Letter-number sequencing). The standard deviation range of the working-memory measures is relatively narrow, and because the upper range of the distribution still falls below 10 (population mean line), we can predict that a significant majority of the sample (at least 84 per cent) have working-memory abilities below the population average (of 10). These estimates match the measures' scores because 83.3 per cent of the sample have a digit span score below 10 and 80.4 per cent of the sample have a letter-number sequencing score below 10.

Correlations within the WAIS

To examine the shared variance (correlation) between the 10 subtests of the WAIS, the scores were correlated and are presented in Table 3.1. Note that the correlations in bold are between the subtests comprising the four cognitive indices of the WAIS-IV.

The strongest correlations, as expected, are between the subtests comprising the four cognitive indices (in bold). All correlations are statistically significant at the high level ($p < .001$), indicating we can be at least 99 per cent confident that there is a correlation between all these subtest scores. It is a matter of the strength of these scores and what these patterns can tell us.

The strongest pairwise correlations are between the verbal comprehension index subtests (Similarities (S), Vocabulary (V), and Information (I)), while the weakest is between Block design (BD) and Matrix reasoning (MR) of the perceptual reasoning index (PRI). The second lowest inter-index correlation is between the two working-memory subtests, Digit span (DS) and Letter-number sequencing (LNS).

Table 3.1 Correlations between the 10 subtest scores of the WAIS-IV (letter-number sequencing rather than arithmetic) within the adult dyslexic client sample.

	S	V	I	BD	MR	VP	DS	LNS	SS
V	.718**	–							
I	.615**	.692**	–						
BD	.307**	.261**	.344**	–					
MR	.290**	.251**	.285**	.563**	–				
VP	.320**	.279**	.353**	.675**	.568**	–			
DS	.329**	.304**	.291**	.313**	.271**	.266**	–		
LNS	.228**	.285**	.265**	.219**	.178**	.201**	.565**	–	
SS	.187**	.138**	.165**	.340**	.265**	.332**	.239**	.188**	–
C	.193**	.167**	.176**	.330**	.298**	.312**	.292**	.265**	.638**

** Correlation is significant at the 0.01 level (1-tailed).

The strongest correlation between two subtests not within the same index (between the Information (I) and Visual puzzles (VP) subtests ($r = .353$)) is still much weaker than the weakest correlation between two subtest scores within the same index (Block design (BD) and Matrix reasoning (MR) ($r = .563$)). The weakest correlation between two subtests is between Vocabulary (V) and Symbol search (SS) ($r = .138$).

Comparison of Measures by Occupation and Sex

Figure 3.6 shows the mean scores and CIs (95 per cent) for each of the core subtests of the WAIS for the client sample.

The means and CIs appear remarkably similar; however, this should not be surprising given that the distinction between university or work referral is likely to be somewhat circumstantial. Generally, universities have become much better at referring students for assessment in recent decades; however, the kinds of employers who support

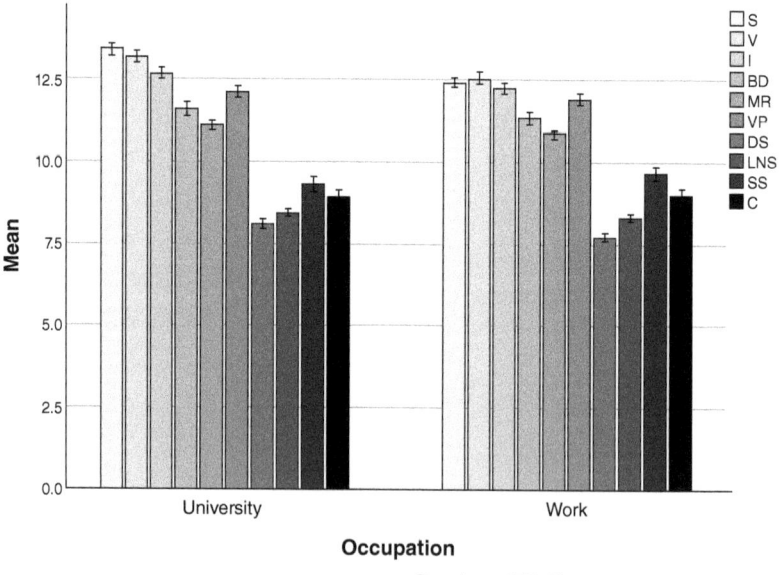

FIGURE 3.6 Sample mean scores for the WAIS-IV subtests comparing the education (university) and employment (work) groups.

staff referral for neurodevelopmental disorders such as dyslexia are likely to be those who are expected to recruit graduates.

The employment group is significantly older than the education group. To assess whether the occupation groups were distinct in character, analyses were carried out to detect significant differences between these groups. In addition, these investigations were combined with an analysis of possible sex differences in performance on the WAIS subtests (there were no expected differences in the general population). However, there could have been interactions between the occupation group and the sex group if there were differences of opportunity or access.

The analyses of the individual subtest scores and indices by participant sex and occupation status are presented in the appendix at the end of this book. Only the vocabulary subtest demonstrated an interaction between sex and occupation. This was the result of males in employment scoring much lower than males in education; however, the effect size is quite small ($\eta_p^2 = .006$) and indicates that this could be treated as a false positive effect. The same pattern, though less pronounced, is seen with the verbal comprehension index score, and the effect is half the size of the Vocabulary effect.

Eight of the 10 subtests indicate there are significant sex differences; Matrix reasoning and Letter-number sequencing have no sex differences. In six subtests where there was a difference, females score higher than males (Information, Digit span, Vocabulary, similarities, Visual puzzles, and Block design). The two exceptions where males score higher than females are symbol search and coding. The largest effect of sex is for the Information subtest ($\eta_p^2 = .027$), which is more than twice as large as the next largest effect size for the Block design ($\eta_p^2 = .013$) and Visual puzzles ($\eta_p^2 = .012$) subtests.

This pattern is replicated for the index scores in which processing speed is the only index that shows a significant male advantage, whereas the other three indices show a female advantage.

Five of the 10 subtests show a significant difference between participants who were assessed while in education and those who were assessed while in employment. The Symbol search subtest shows an advantage for those in employment over those in education, while the other four show an advantage for those assessed at university. The Similarities effect is the strongest main effect ($\eta_p^2 = .033$) for occupation and is the strongest effect found in all the subtest and index analyses. The effect for Similarities is over four times stronger than the next highest effect for Vocabulary ($\eta_p^2 = .008$).

Latent Structure

There is a method called factor analysis that helps to identify the relationships between multiple measures. These relationships can involve more than two measures, which makes this method more powerful than correlation analysis (which can only measure the relationship between pairs of measures). The relationships are hidden from direct observation and so are referred to as latent variables. We can carry out a factor analysis to see how many of these latent variables there are and how the measures relate to them. We refer to the latent variables as factors. If we believe that we know how many latent variables exist within the data, we carry out a confirmatory factor analysis (CFA) to look for and explore this number of factors. However, if we are unsure about how many latent variables exist within the data, we carry out an exploratory factor analysis (EFA).

There are two steps to factor analysis. First is the extraction, where a set number (CFA) or unknown number (EFA) of factors are identified (extracted). The most common method of carrying out this step is a process called principal component analysis (PCA). The second step is called rotation, and this is carried out to make the extracted factors interpretable, the way in which the measures relate to the factors. There are two main types of rotation: orthogonal and oblique. Orthogonal rotation assumes the factors are uncorrelated (the most common methods are varimax, quartimax, and equamax). Oblique rotation enables factors to be correlated (the most common methods are promax and direct oblimin). Orthogonal rotation has tended to be used in psychometric measures of personality where we want to find the number and character of distinct (uncorrelated) measures of personality (e.g. the five-factor model of personality, also known as the Big Five). Oblique rotation has been used in psychometric measures of ability where we understand that there is a strong general intelligence measure (little g) influencing the subtypes (e.g. verbal and non-verbal or concrete and fluid).

Psychometric measures of ability such as the WAIS are refined using factor analysis. As noted earlier, the WAIS has a particular structure (verbal and non-verbal, concrete, and information processing). The WAIS has a four-factor structure represented by the four indices; it was designed to have these indices and so would have been refined using CFA.

We carried out an EFA on the 10 subtests. This was exploratory because we did not want to assume that each of the subtest scores would load in the expected pattern (linked to their respective indices) because of the specific sample we are exploring, adults attending a dyslexia assessment. We can conceptualise this as exploring the patterns of responses to the WAIS within this sample of adults with dyslexia.

These are the technical points for transparency. A PCA was conducted, and three components were extracted that cumulatively explained 67.98 per cent of the variance in the sample's scores on the 10 WAIS subtests. A promax rotation with Kaiser normalisation was performed. This is an oblique rotation and is used because it is expected that the component factors will be correlated (because of the effect of general ability). The pattern matrix of this rotation is presented in Table 3.2 along with the variance explained by each factor. Factor loadings below .30 have been hidden, and those over .50 have been emboldened to aid interpretability.

It is important to note that this analysis was conducted to establish whether the patterns of difficulties within a sample of people with dyslexia correspond to the pattern that would be expected in a typical sample (the four factors representing the four indices of the WAIS-IV). Table 3.2 shows that they do not follow the same pattern as expected from the structure of the WAIS because three factors were found.

Table 3.2 *Factor analysis pattern matrix of the 10 WAIS-IV subtests for the sample of dyslexic clients.*

	Factors		
	1	2	3
Variance explained	39.70%	15.99%	12.29%
Visual puzzles	.840		
Block design	.819		
Matrix reasoning	.785		
Vocabulary		.869	
Similarities		.805	
Information		.800	
Letter-number sequencing			.826
Digit span			.756
Coding	.362		.605
Symbol search	.427		.507

When we talk about how a measure relates to a factor, we refer to it as 'loading' on a factor. You can consider this as equivalent to correlating with the factor. As expected, all factor loadings are positive, indicating that clients who tend to score higher on one subtest loading on a factor also tend to score higher on the other factor loading subtests and vice versa.

The perceptual reasoning index (PRI) is accounted for by factor 1; all three subtests are strongly loaded on this factor. Likewise, the verbal comprehension index (VCI) is accounted for by factor 2; however, it's noteworthy that factor 2 accounts for less than half the variance of factor 1. This may be a result of factor 1 having the two processing speed subtests loading on it, although at a much lower level than the perceptual reasoning subtests. This means that factor 1 can appear to be a much more coherent factor.

Factor 3 contains the four fluid ability subtests comprising the two information-processing indices, working memory (WMI) and processing speed (PSI). The two working-memory subtests are the strongest loading (Letter-number sequencing and Digit span) and the two processing-speed subtests are weaker loading (Coding and Symbol search). The two processing-speed subtests also load on factor 1, but at a weaker level than factor 3. This indicates that factor 3 appears to represent the information processing and fluid ability measures combined. This construct appears to be similar to the cognitive proficiency index (CPI), which is an aggregate of the four fluid ability measures of the WAIS. The CPI can be compared with the concrete ability index, called the general ability index (GAI), to establish whether there are general information-processing difficulties (beyond working memory or aspects of working memory alone). The two working-memory subtests load the strongest on this factor; however, this is also because the processing-speed subtest scores have been split between factor 1 and factor 3, thereby diminishing their impact on factor 3. This also means that the verbal ability measures are split between two factors, factor 2 representing the concrete verbal abilities and factor 3 including, but not limited to, the verbal information-processing abilities (working memory).

It would be useful to know whether visual working memory would align more with factor 1 or factor 3. However, there is not a visual working-memory measure within the core subtest set of the WAIS-IV. An example of a visual working-memory measure is the Symbol span subtest from the Wechsler Memory Scales (American Psychiatric Association, 2009). Symbol span was developed as a visual analogue to the digit span subtest within the WAIS-IV.

Table 3.3 shows the correlations between the three factors extracted in this analysis. Because we used an oblique method of rotation, the factors extracted in the factor analysis are potentially

Table 3.3 *Correlations between the three oblique factors extracted from the dyslexic client sample.*

	Factor 1 (PRI)	Factor 2 (VCI)
Factor 2 (VCI)	.248	
Factor 3 (CPI)	.412	.235

correlated, and these are shown in Table 3.3. Given that the two processing-speed subtests are shared between factor 1 and factor 3, it is not surprising that there is shared variance between these two factors.

Rapid Naming

Rapid naming has been shown to be a correlate of reading skills but also has implications for language abilities such as word finding. The rapid naming of colours, objects, letters, and digits tests used were from the Comprehensive Test of Phonological Processing (CTOPP) (Wagner et al., 1999), the first edition, as colour and object naming were discontinued in the second edition, even though both have been shown to relate to verbal and written language skills.

Table 3.4 shows that the strongest correlations are, as expected, between the rapid-naming measures: they range from .597 (between object and digit naming) to .843 (between colour and object naming).

Table 3.5 shows that the strongest correlations outside of the rapid-naming set are between Proofreading and Spelling (.342),

Table 3.4 *Correlations between the rapid-naming measures.*

Rapid naming	Colours	Objects	Letters
Objects	.843**	–	
Letters	.729**	.712**	–
Digits	.662**	.597**	.767**

* = $p < .05$, ** = $p < .01$

Table 3.5 *Correlations between the literacy skill measures.*

	Reading speed	Writing speed	Spelling
Writing speed	.319**	–	
Spelling	.082**	.080**	–
Proofreading	.285**	.319**	.342**

* = $p < .05$, ** = $p < .01$

Proofreading and Writing speed (.319), and Silent-reading speed and Writing speed (.319).

Table 3.6 shows the relationship between the four rapid-naming measures, the two working-memory subtests of the WAIS, and the literacy skill measures. The Digit span subtest is correlated with all four rapid-naming measures, the strongest with Digit naming (.168) and the weakest with Object naming (.077). Letter-number sequencing only correlates relatively weakly with Colour naming and Digit naming (both .069). The strongest relationship between the rapid-naming measures is with Writing speed (all are statistically significant).

Literacy Skills

The literacy assessments are taken from multiple sources and are broadly focused on aspects of reading and writing skills. Table 3.5 shows the correlations between the key literacy measures. The correlations are Spearman's correlations because some of the measures are ordinal and some other scale measures are not normally distributed.

The SDRT (1983) has four ordinal rankings, professional being the highest, followed by technical, vocational, and functional, for oral-reading accuracy and comprehension. The silent-reading speed is also taken from the SDRT. Proofreading and the York writing speed are taken from the YAA-R (Warmington et al., 2012). The spelling scale is taken from the WIAT-III (Wechsler, 2017).

Limitations

The most obvious limitation of the results described is that they are based on archive research and there is, therefore, no control group. Nevertheless, it can be argued that individuals in the sample described here are being compared with those who made up the standardisation population described in the test manual for WAIS-

Table 3.6 Correlations between the rapid-naming measures and the literacy skill measures.

Rapid naming	Digit span	Letter-number sequencing	Silent-reading speed	Writing speed	Spelling	Proofreading
Colours	.149** [.085, .213]	.069* [.004, .134]	.037 [−.029, .103]	.187** [.122, .251]	−.028 [−.094, .038]	.064* [−.003, .130]
Objects	.077* [.012, .142]	.019 [−.046, .085]	−.045 [−.111, .021]	.098** [.031, .164]	−.039 [−.104, .027]	.038 [−.029, .104]
Digits	.168** [.104, .231]	.069* [.003, .133]	.113* [.047, .177]	.229** [.165, .292]	.002 [−.064, .068]	.095* [.029, .161]
Letters	.126** [.061, .189]	.002 [−.064, .067]	.090** [.025, .155]	.228** [.163, .291]	−.006 [−.072, .060]	.084** [.018, .150]

* = $p < .05$, ** = $p < .01$

IV. In addition, the results outlined reflect the scores of a much larger sample than that relied upon by the authors of the test.

The results demonstrate that a significant number of individuals who are finding aspects of academic study and employment-related tasks challenging experience cognitive difficulties with information-processing tasks related to working memory and processing speed. This is despite them having concrete verbal and non-verbal abilities that should ensure they are able to succeed academically and in the workplace.

IMPLICATIONS FOR A MODEL OF DYSLEXIA

Although slow processing speed is often advanced as a justification for adjustments in assessment and workplace settings, we can see that it correlates with working memory. There is also a relationship between working memory and key literacy skills.

Based on the results presented here, working memory is the most prevalent cognitive weakness experienced by the individuals reporting for assessment. They all meet the ICD-11 criteria for reading disorder and, therefore, have dyslexia. Without arguing for a core-deficit, if we follow the description of working memory outlined earlier, a model based on a deficit in this important cognitive ability can provide an explanation for many of the symptoms reported by individuals with dyslexia. These include aspects of literacy, but also other important everyday skills such as time estimation, memory lapses, and behaviours associated with executive functions such as planning and adaptation to change. It could also account for non-cognitive factors such as anxiety. The data described here is also supportive of language-based activities, such as word finding, being undermined by weak naming ability.

This does not change the long-established approach to differential diagnosis, as establishing inconsistencies in cognitive profiles has been the norm and reinforces the process. There does, however, need to be greater emphasis on the interpretation of these, and the implications for people with dyslexia in domains beyond reading and writing if they are to develop self-understanding as well as greater empathy from those working with them. Acknowledging that working memory is a significant processing problem in dyslexia can lead us towards Lipton's *loveliest explanation*.

SUMMARY

In this chapter we have presented a description and analysis of archive data from 1,423 assessments conducted at our practice. The results demonstrate:

- a consistent pattern of strengths and weaknesses on the Wechsler Adult Intelligence Scale, the latter being in working memory and processing speed;
- weaknesses in rapid naming, correlating with silent-reading speed, spelling, and writing speed;
- that reading comprehension is a persisting problem for people with dyslexia;
- the implications for a model of dyslexia that provides the *loveliest explanation*.

4 Working Memory

INTRODUCTION

Despite the use of the single word to describe them, memories are not all the same. Some allow us to know who we are and where we came from. Others allow us to know where we are going. These are all known as declarative memories, which can take different forms enabling us to recall or recognise people, places, and objects.

The role of memory has been fundamental to information-processing models of neurodevelopmental disorders, short-term, long-term, and working memory being essential to learning, retention, and recall. It was central to the original concept of 'learning disabilities' put forward by Kirk (1962) in which inefficiencies in memory were proposed as disruptive factors between sensory input and behavioural output, but the distinction between the different kinds of memory is often a source of confusion.

SHORT-TERM MEMORY

Short-term memory allows for immediate storage but has a limited finite capacity capable of handling only a small amount of information (Sweller, 2019). Contrary to what has become the meme that we can remember seven pieces of information at a time, fMRI studies have suggested it is only four unless we engage in maintenance strategies such as chunking and rehearsal. We rely on short-term memory to recall sequences such as instructions and telephone numbers (Pinker, 2022). Analogies used to explain short-term memory capacity have included describing it as a shelf with a limited storage facility, but it is better understood as a process rather than a structure (Davelaar, 2013). This might explain why rehearsal and repetition can help with the maintenance of information, so people need to take control over the way it is presented to them.

LONG-TERM MEMORY

Although it is what people forget that worries them, they are thinking of recall rather than retention. Most memory problems relate to the retrieval of information from long-term memory rather than storage. 'Memory is fallible, of course, but not because of storage limitations so much as retrieval limitations' (Levitin, 2014, p. xiv). Long-term memory has unlimited capacity, and the memories within it can remain over the course of an individual's lifespan. It is thought that nearly every conscious experience is stored somewhere in the brain. Within long-term storage, there are essentially two kinds of memory: procedural and declarative.

Procedural

This includes memories related to activities learned through practice and repetition, such as riding a bicycle, driving a car, and typing. These are implicit and rely on parts of the brain such as the cerebellum, motor control areas, and the basal ganglia. It is often referred to as motor-memory.

Declarative

This kind of memory is for facts, rules, events, definitions, people, places, and experiences that someone can recall when necessary. It is available in consciousness and falls into two categories:

- Episodic memory: this relates to specific events, typically with autobiographical content. It allows individuals to learn, store, and retrieve information about unique personal experiences and events that occur in daily life, including content and context. Time has a central role in the process of retrieval of an experience, that is, the ability to remember the order of events that composed the episode.

- Semantic memory: this includes knowledge about the world. For example, Rome is the capital of Italy, the latter providing context, as well as syntax or the set of rules for the generation of structures such as sentences.

WORKING MEMORY

In a TED talk Doolittle (2013) stated that life comes at us very quickly, and one of the abilities that enables us to make sense of the world is working memory. We process what we learn, and if we are not processing, we are not living. You can't turn working memory off; if you do, you are in a coma.

There are many descriptions of working memory, but they have in common the notion that it is a combination of transient memory and long-term memory, the system that holds mental representations available for processing (Oberauer et al., 2016). It is thought to control attention, allow one to remember instructions, keep in mind a plan of things to do, and to help solve complex problems (Klingberg, 2009). Working memory is of limited capacity, a bottleneck that restricts our ability to process information and reason. It is a core component of higher cognitive functions, that is, the ability to maintain and manipulate information over a period of seconds (Constantinidis & Klingberg, 2016), and is a system fundamental to effective performance in learning and work settings, and an important mechanism of general cognitive ability. Essentially, it allows for taking in, manipulating, and storing information for problem solving in the immediate, retrieving information from long-term memory, and combining the two. People who have strong working-memory ability can be good storytellers, do well on standardised tests, have advanced levels of writing skill, and can reason at high levels. High working-memory capacity has been associated with expertise in activities such as sight-reading music, as well as playing chess (Arthur et al., 2021).

In summary and at its simplest level, working memory can be thought of as the interaction between short-term and long-term memory. It is a dynamic system, but its functions can be described as:

- holding on to information provided by the senses in the very short term;
- entering information for effective storage and retrieval in long-term memory;
- enabling the recall of information from long-term memory on demand;
- allowing the above to happen simultaneously.

At a language level it can be thought of as being able to multitask with words, both verbally and in the written form (Mcloughlin & Leather, 2013).

The use of the terms working memory and working-memory capacity vary across a range of research fields. Wilhelm et al. (2013) distinguish between working memory referring to a hypothetical cognitive system responsible for providing access to information required for ongoing cognitive processes, and working-memory capacity denoting an individual differences construct, reflecting the limited capacity of a person's working memory. To some extent we are using the terms interchangeably, but the emphasis here is on the practical, so mainly the individual differences construct. Working-memory capacity is determined by how we negotiate; we need to process information as it happens, repeat, think, talk, practise, elaborate, and illustrate thinking. We need to envelop existing knowledge around new knowledge and use imagery. In evolutionary terms, working memory is a tool genetically adapted to cope with increasingly complex environments. It is not just about the past but holding together the present in mind so people can learn, make decisions, and solve problems. It has been the focus of extensive research efforts because it plays a central role in several aspects of cognition, including language comprehension, fluid intelligence, writing, arithmetic, and problem solving. Most human activities involve working memory at some level, and most major information-processing models of skill acquisition and learning include it as a component. There is some consensus amongst psychologists that the processes attributed to working memory are essential in human cognition. That is, one must keep information in mind while processing it to function intellectually and socially. It has been referred to as the gatekeeper of learning (Peavler, 2024).

WORKING MEMORY AND DYSLEXIA

In dyslexia research there has been a particular interest in working memory. Amongst the many and diverse theories that have been proposed for the cause of dyslexia are those that have been 'described within the framework of multiple memory systems, with links to neural and cognitive substrates of language' (Démonet et al., 2004, p. 1451). It has been proposed that neurodevelopmental disorders such as dyslexia can result from an impairment in working memory that persists across the lifespan (Eloranta et al., 2019). It has also been suggested that its impact extends beyond literacy, having a significant effect on planning, problem solving, acting under novel situations in learning, and social and work settings (McLoughlin & Leather, 2013). This implies that people with dyslexia are likely to need appropriate support across a range of behaviours if they are to achieve their full potential in education, employment, and life generally (Smith-Spark & Fisk, 2007).

A limited-capacity working-memory system can explain the academic problems experienced by people with dyslexia. Although some individuals with learning disorders have deficits related to phonological processing, they also experience problems with executive functions. This is consistent with theorists who adopt a resource-interaction approach in which individual differences emerge when academic processes compete for a limited supply of resources. Working memory becomes overloaded if it must process too much information at the same time. Performance in lower-order processing abilities can impact on executive dysfunctions in addition to problems with storage (Smith-Spark & Fisk, 2007). Although a comparative study showed that the only difference in executive functions between people with dyslexia and those without was in the inability to inhibit irrelevant context (Brosnan et al., 2002), there is evidence for impairments in everyday cognition amongst people with dyslexia, including cognitive failures (Smith-Spark et al., 2004; Leather et al., 2011; Protopapa & Smith-Spark, 2022).

Working-memory impairments have been related to specific aspects of reading disorders. Of particular interest has been reading comprehension, so it is of some significance that amongst the sample described in Chapter 3, this was the weakest literacy skill. Whether this is an intrinsic difficulty has been the subject of debate, it having been suggested that, consistent with bidirectional theories of neural connectivity, the inefficiency of lower-level phonological processes may place additional demands on working memory, leading to cognitive overload (Peavler, 2024). Consequently, fewer resources are available for higher-level processes involved in comprehension such as extracting information from text to elaborate on meaning.

THE BADDELEY MODEL OF WORKING MEMORY

There are different models of working memory, including the embedded-process model (Cowan, 2012) and the multicomponent system proposed by Baddeley (1986, 2000, 2007, 2010; Baddeley & Hitch, 2007). Although they have much in common, including the role of focused attention and executive control, we rely on the latter. It is probably the best known, it has clarity, and it is the most comprehensive. It has been extended to apply to usual and disordered language, in both verbal and written domains, as well as learning generally. Baddeley has also adapted it to apply to emotional development (2010). It was primarily developed from research based on adult samples and then generalised to the performance of children. Baddeley (1992, p. 556) wrote that the term working memory 'refers to the brain system that provides temporary storage and manipulation of the information necessary for such complex cognitive tasks as language comprehension, learning and reasoning'. He originally proposed three components: the phonological loop, the visual-spatial sketchpad, and the central executive. The first two are limited-capacity passive slave systems used for the temporary storage of information, and the third coordinates activity. Each of these and their functions are described here.

The *phonological loop* contains the articulatory control system, which can hold information by articulating it subvocally, and the phonological store, which holds speech-based information, both components relying on phonological coding. The phonological loop has been associated with linguistic models of dyslexia as it underlies phonological processing and is necessary for the temporary storage of new words while they are being remembered, preserving the order of words, grammar, and syntax, as well as language learning generally. It has been suggested that it is indistinguishable from phonological deficits, which have been the dominant explanation for literacy difficulties. Its function is to facilitate the acquisition of new words. It has, therefore, been shown to be important in the development of literacy skills.

Phonological processing is the use of the sounds of a language to process spoken and written language. It includes phonological awareness, phonological working memory, and phonological retrieval. All three components are important for speech production, as well as the development of spoken and written language skills. Phonological awareness is the awareness of the sounds of a language and the ability to consciously analyse and manipulate the structure. It is an umbrella term, phonemic awareness applying to the units being manipulated, phonemes rather than words or syllables. Phonological working memory involves storing phonemic information in short-term memory. This information is then available for manipulation during phonological awareness tasks.

Phonological retrieval is the ability to recall the phonemes associated with specific graphemes. Phonological memory is the ability to hold on to speech-based information in short-term memory. We rely heavily on this when reading and spelling. It is also thought to be related to a range of abilities including:

- remembering serial information generally;
- following instructions;
- remembering the alphabet and telephone numbers;
- recalling the order of letters in words;
- pronouncing multisyllabic words;
- time estimation;
- language learning generally.

In the dataset presented in Chapter 3, the phonological loop was measured by digit span and letter-number sequencing from the WAIS-IV.

The *visual-spatial sketchpad* processes visual and spatial information, receiving both from visual perception and retrieval from long-term memory in the form of images. It has generally been less well understood than the phonological loop, but it is thought to store images of the visual appearance of objects and scenes. It has been suggested that, like the phonological loop, it might contain two systems – the visual cache and the spatial scribe – and is responsible for:

- the storage and manipulation of spatial and visual information;
- storing form and colour information;
- retaining spatial/movement information.

In the data presented in Chapter 3, the WAIS-IV measures grouped under perceptual reasoning can be considered to involve the visual-spatial sketchpad.

The *central executive* interacts with the two passive storage systems used for temporary storage of different classes of information. The speech-based phonological loop and the visual-spatial sketchpad are both in direct contact with the central executive, which coordinates activity within the cognitive system, but also devotes some of its resources to increasing the amount of information that can be held in the two slave systems (Baddeley & Logie, 1999). It provides higher-order control processing, including attentional control, multitasking, retrieval strategy switching, selective inhibition, and mental manipulation (Shura et al., 2016). The central executive allows for:

- maintaining attention;
- resisting interference such as distractions;
- changing strategies;
- planning;
- organisation;
- time estimation.

To some extent, Baddeley's use of the term *executive* muddied the water as to whether there is a distinction between the central executive and frontal lobe abilities that control executive functions generally. The latter are complex, and so is their measurement, mostly focusing on transfer and generalisation tasks that test the ability to change cognitive strategies automatically according to demands.

The *episodic buffer* is a component added to the original model of working memory (Baddeley, 2000). This is thought to facilitate access to long-term memory and binds together the other components. Access is through awareness, taking people from unconscious compensation to conscious compensation, and providing a rationale for the need to develop metacognitive skills. It allows for the important strategy of 'chunking' to increase attentional capacity by collapsing related data together. Its functions can be described as:

- coordination of the interaction between control processes and the dependent slave systems;
- integrating information from a range of sources into a single structure or 'episode';
- acting as an intermediary between the central executive, the phonological loop, and the visual-spatial sketchpad.

The principal mode of retrieval from the episodic buffer is conscious awareness, so measurement might involve evaluating metacognitive skills.

The *hedonic detector* is the most recent addition to the model (Baddeley, 2007; Baddeley et al., 2012). Hedonic adaptation is the psychological process by which people become accustomed to stimuli that produce emotional effects over time. It occurs in response to both positive and negative experiences. Multiple mechanisms are presumed to underlie hedonic adaptation, including cognitive processes such as attention, goals and values, perceptions, aspirations, explanations, and social-temporal comparisons (Lyubomirsky, 2011).

Baddeley hypothesised that the hedonic detector picks up positive or negative associations from the episodic component of working memory. He was influenced by the valence world hypothesis in which *valence* is the psychological value of an object, event, person, or goal in an individual's life. Negative valence is towards things that should be avoided, and positive valence towards things that should be sought after. It is assumed that the world we perceive and recall is not emotionally neutral and that its features are positively or negatively weighted, suggesting that associations can influence working memory and attention, the experiences of them being held within it.

Everyday choices can be rapid and possibly automatic complex decisions but are heavily reliant on working memory to process stimuli that must be evaluated, and the result maintained while others are established, and the results compared. Baddeley cites the work of Damasio (1996) in which it is suggested that the failure to sense the positive and negative nature of potential outcomes can influence decision making. Thus, there is an assumption that there is a hedonic detection system capable of assessing stimuli. This would require both temporary storage and the capacity to manipulate information, implying the involvement of working memory. Baddeley et al. (2012) suggest that that evaluation system would have five crucial features:

- a neutral point on the valence scale – readings above that point reflecting a positive valence and those below it a negative valence;
- a sensitivity and stability if there are to be consistency of action over time or a capacity to direct change from that level;
- a capacity to average across several features of each potential action, requiring memory storage;
- a capacity to discriminate between stored options;
- acknowledgement that the manipulation and judgement of hedonic information is likely to depend on working memory, particularly the central executive component.

According to this description of the hedonic detector, social adjustment difficulties including anxiety and depression could stem from a hedonic evaluation problem, that is, the failure to discriminate between the positive and the negative. Working memory is an important tool in evaluating the options of responding in different situations appropriately, and the hedonic detector is part of that system, its function being to evaluate the environment, including past experiences and plans. When these are negative, the signal is negative, leading to rumination and a search for a solution. Baddeley has suggested that, if a solution is not apparent, depressive passivity might develop, and that the detector system will look for an internal explanation, 'leading to self-blame and retrieval of negative rather than positive self-schemata leading to further depression' (2007, p. 292).

It can be assumed that, as with cognition, the relationship between executive functions and emotion is bidirectional, operating in an interactive manner. An imbalance in the working-memory system and accessing negative episodes might, therefore, be one of the reasons why people with dyslexia are at risk of experiencing more anxiety and depression than others. It is because of their cognitive make-up, not just a response to their life experiences. This does not mean that their past will be insignificant, but, if we follow Baddeley's argument, people with dyslexia are more likely to access their negative rather than their positive experiences of learning, working, and life in general. Non-cognitive difficulties are not part of the common understanding of dyslexia and are more likely to be attributed to motivation, attitude, and application, contributing to misunderstanding and a lack of support. Although it is largely a hypothetical construct, it seems reasonable to assume that people whose working-memory ability is inefficient are at risk of focusing on the negative, an important implication for interventions such as counselling. It must be acknowledged by those supporting individuals with dyslexia.

Damasio (1996) proposed that an emotion is a bodily response to a mental image, and the feeling of an emotion is a cognitive response to the resultant bodily condition, explaining disturbances or uneasiness. The theory proved attractive because of the suggestion that there are a rational part of the brain and an emotional part, and the former without the latter is deficient in optimal decision making. This had considerable appeal, but Hacker (2017) suggests that the argument is confused, for 'if better means optimally rational and if the emotional part of the brain evaluates options better than the rational parts of the brain, then the so-called emotional parts are the rational parts' (p. 110).

There is a two-way interaction between factors such as fatigue and stress and the efficiency of working memory. Anxiety, for example, is thought to restrict working-memory capacity (Moran, 2016; Lisica et al., 2022). Although mild stress can enhance cognitive functioning on some memory tasks, there is a point at which it can become debilitating (Sandi, 2013). The evidence for the negative effects of acute in-the-moment stress on working-memory capacity is sound (Goller et al., 2020). People with dyslexia will have problems with tasks that place demands on working memory, and these will be greater when they are under duress. In general, people who have mental health problems show impaired working-memory capacity when affective or emotional material is present (Schweizer et al., 2019).

THE NEUROLOGY OF WORKING MEMORY

The limbic system is where memory begins. It includes the hippocampus, amygdalae, and the hypothalamus. It is the seat of our emotions, as well as behaviour, motivation, and long-term memory. The hypothalamus regulates basic emotions. Here also are behaviour, motivation, and long-term memory. In the hippocampus we experience the space around us, sounds, and images. It triggers the amygdalae, of which there are two – left and right. They perform a primary role in processing memory and emotional reactions. The senses feed information into the amygdalae. Memories are encoded in long-term memory storage through a chain of biochemical and cellular processes in the hippocampus and the temporal lobe.

The hippocampus and surrounding areas form a medial temporal system that plays a crucial role in episodic memory

(Benarroch, 2021). The hippocampal circuits provide a spatial and temporal framework for relating experiences, creating a cognitive map based on individual autobiographical events. The temporally organised activity of hippocampal neurones helps organise memories in space and time.

In Hagoort's (2017) unification and control model, it was proposed that different areas of the temporal cortex store information about word form, meanings, and syntactic templates that have been laid down in memory during language acquisition and form the building blocks of language comprehension and production. They interact with areas in the frontal gyrus, including Broca's area and the adjacent cortex. The dorsolateral prefrontal cortex and the anterior cingulate cortex are involved in executive control of these operations.

Both short-term and long-term memory are thought to be stored in the hippocampus and the prefrontal cortex, but as should be evident from Chapter 2, the brain is a very complex organ, and it would be naïve to assume that memories are not distributed throughout its structure.

The maintenance of working memory results from the interaction between selective attentional processing of sensory information and representations in long-term memory. These involve loops between frontal and posterior cortical encoded perceptual information, as well as subcortical structures such as the basal ganglia and the cerebellum. There are multiple working-memory network interactions that involve precise timing mechanisms in goal-directed working memory, which appear to include cerebellar circuits that activate during learning, and automatisation can influence the level of skill development in any of the functional language systems (Nicolson & Fawcett, 2019).

SUMMARY

The main points this chapter can be summarised as follows.

- We have emphasised the role of memory in explaining developmental learning disorders such as dyslexia.

- There has been an elaboration of working memory based on the model developed by Baddeley.
- The relationship between working memory and literacy has been described.
- We have drawn out the broader implications of having a working-memory impairment, including the impact on executive functions.
- We have included a consideration of the relationship between working memory and non-cognitive factors such as anxiety.

5   Rapid Naming

INTRODUCTION

A meta-analysis of published research studies comparing children and adults who have a reading disability with their average-reading counterparts found that three cognitive variables across a wide range play a key role in differentiating the two groups: phonological awareness, verbal memory, and rapid-naming ability (Swanson & Hsieh, 2009). The first two can be attributed to differences in the phonological loop component of working memory, but although much of the literature on rapid-naming ability includes it as a component of phonological processing, there is increasing evidence to suggest that it is not the same, so it merits separate attention.

RAPID NAMING

Rapid naming is a cognitive construct referring to processing speed and executive control in language access. It is related to lexical access, the automaticity of verbal encoding, and producing verbal information. Being able to name symbols and objects, associating images with words, is fundamental to language development, both spoken and written. It is a more complex process than it might seem as 'from the perception and recognition of a stimulus as familiar, to obtaining semantic information about this stimulus, accessing a mental representation, and finally executing its name our brain engages in a series of dissociable yet interacting stages to name objects' (Gleichgerrcht et al., 2015, p. 292). As mentioned in Chapter 4, for most of us retrieval is more difficult than storage in memory, so word finding can be undermined. The technical name for it is lethologica, and word finding becomes harder as we age, over the life course, at around one second per decade up to 55 years (Wiig et al., 2007).

RAPID NAMING AND DYSLEXIA

Rapid automatic naming (RAN) has been identified as a significant process in the development of reading skills. It is thought to predict aspects of current and future reading skill development, including text accuracy, fluency, and comprehension. In the past it has been regarded as an aspect of phonological processing and is included in measures of that ability such as the CTOPP (Wagner et al., 1999, 2013). RAN has, therefore, been considered a component of working memory. It is, however, related to but separate from phonological processing. Wolf and Bowers (1999) suggested that the phonological core hypothesis explanation of reading difficulties is incomplete, proposing a double-deficit hypothesis, difficulties with slow naming speed being independent of phonological skills.

Measures of RAN provide information about an individual's ability to retrieve words quickly and easily from long-term memory. People with poor RAN, and therefore difficulties with word retrieval, tend to have weaknesses in reading and writing fluency regardless of their general language ability. The data described in Chapter 3 showed that rapid naming was a consistent weakness, particularly the naming of objects, and that this was related to silent-reading speed. Rapid automatic naming correlates with skills such as the automaticity of reading accuracy and comprehension. A meta-analytic study of adults with a reading disorder showed a significant rapid-naming deficit (Reis et al., 2020), which was consistent with earlier work. Having conducted another meta-analytic study, Araújo and Faísca (2019) concluded that individuals with dyslexia experience rapid-naming difficulties that are expressed by slower naming times in response to familiar items; these findings are pervasive and become even more prominent with ageing than other effects of dyslexia. They argued that there is strong support for substantial impairment in RAN amongst individuals with dyslexia compared with typically developing controls of the same chronological age. The size of the deficit was associated with the severity of reading impairment; that is, the slower a participant's reading fluency level, the slower their naming speed.

Difficulties with naming often become apparent later in adolescence and adulthood, and comparative as well as longitudinal studies have shown naming speed to be a persisting problem (Callens et al., 2014; Eloranta et al., 2019). They can be evidenced as memory lapses, forgetting the names of objects and proper names, and malapropisms. They are not Freudian slips linked to suppressed or repressed urges. Rapid automatic naming is influenced by processing speed, working memory, associative memory, and long-term verbal memory (Mazur-Mosiewicz & Davis, 2011). At a cognitive level, relative to age-matched controls, readers with dyslexia perform poorer in rapid naming across languages, irrespective of the orthography in which they learn to read. The transparency of the writing system does not influence the size of the deficit, and neither does the type of writing system. Boets et al. (2013) demonstrated that even high-functioning adult readers with dyslexia were impaired on an object-naming task, which reflects a difficulty in accessing and outputting more general information from the visual stimulus.

Poor rapid naming is a long-term and universal symptom of dyslexia, and the transparency of the writing system does not influence its severity. Rapid automatic naming is an important system in all languages and writing systems. However, it might be that item pause time constitutes the main source of naming difficulties in dyslexia, whereas the articulation time is unrelated to measures of reading. The underlying deficit in dyslexia significantly affects the naming of items in both serial and discrete task formats, albeit with a somewhat greater impairment for the former. Because readers are inefficient at naming in both serial and discrete formats, it can be concluded that the impairment is at least partly related to the underlying cognitive processes required for naming and is not simply associated with difficulties in serial performance. Low naming speed, therefore, is not just a matter of task complexity but represents a core measurable feature of dyslexia and its diagnosis.

Readers with dyslexia are significantly impaired in RAN tasks of non-alphanumeric data, which eliminates the possibility that some aspects peculiar to letters are only responsible for the delays in rapid naming (it is unfortunate that the revised second edition of the CTOPP in 2013 removed rapid naming of objects and colours retaining only digits and letters). It is unlikely that the phonological component of RAN performance and in particular the phonological problems that feature in dyslexia are associated with the encoding and retrieval stages of rapid naming. Research results have shown that having more and different items to be named does not predict group differences. Slower rapid naming has been found to persist into adulthood, including in high-functioning participants who can read.

The rapid-naming deficit is mainly expressed in abnormally long response times and generalises across stimulus types: pictures, colours, letters, and numbers (for example, as measured using the CTOPP, 1999). Slower than expected rapid naming is an important symptom of dyslexia in all languages and diagnostic systems. Rapid naming is a strong correlate of reading ability and reliably discriminates between readers with dyslexia and those without, independent of age. It should be noted that, as in serial rapid naming, not all discrete naming tasks are the same and their relationship with reading is a complex one, because it potentially varies across development. An open issue is whether the naming deficit that features in dyslexia has a causal influence on the disorder or is also influenced by a lack of reading experience, given that reading experience fosters faster access to phonological representations in RAN. There is evidence of similar scores on measures of rapid naming amongst individuals with dyslexia and typically developing readers who have the same absolute level of reading skill. This result is, however, ambiguous as it could mean that underlying differences in rapid naming exist between the two groups, but they are concealed by the fact that the older participants with dyslexia have better metacognitive strategies or higher overall processing speed. Nevertheless, the inclusion of RAN tasks in neuro-psychological educational assessments of reading disorders is essential for the reasons outlined earlier.

BEYOND LITERACY

Miles (1983) wrote that 'the reading and spelling problems of a dyslexic person are part of a wider disability which shows itself whenever symbolic material has to be identified and named' (p. 98). One of the better examples of the failure to infer from evidence of implications beyond literacy is seen with rapid naming. That it is associated with reading and spelling is well established, but it does have other functions, including the development of oral language skills. It is, for example, related to word finding, and Snowling et al. (2012) found that people who self-reported as having dyslexia rated themselves as having more difficulty with word-finding tasks. Being able to find words is essential to verbal and written communication. As Momaday (1987) has suggested, the first word gives origin to the second, the first and second to the third, and the third to the fourth, and so on. You cannot begin with the second word.

Dysnomia (or anomic aphasia), a difficulty with recalling and using words, leads to people struggling to express ideas verbally, even though they know the meaning of what they want to say. It taps semantic memory, and if we understand dyslexia as being part of a wider language disability, it has implications for remembering people's names, as well as identifying directions such as right and left. Therefore, there is no such thing as 'directional dyslexia'; it is not a problem with spatial orientation but one of labelling due to the naming difficulty. Rapid naming has also been associated with 'tip-of-the-tongue' recall, the lethologica referred to earlier wherein a person has difficulty recalling the word to use even though they clearly comprehend the intended meaning. Faust and Sharfstein-Friedman (2003) found that adolescents with dyslexia produced more tip-of-the-tongue responses, made more substitutions, and benefited less from phonological cues on a picture-naming task. It was concluded that adolescents with dyslexia have significant naming difficulties that seem to arise because of a difficulty in accessing the phonological word forms. In verbal communication, people who have dyslexia produce significantly more errors and tip-of-the-tongue responses (Faust & Sharfstein-Friedman, 2003). These difficulties can leave people feeling socially awkward and unintelligent, resulting in their self-confidence being undermined. There are also consequences for verbal communication that can impact on interpersonal skills and social relationships. Forgetting the names of people one has met many times can also be a source of embarrassment.

Naming problems can also affect seemingly simple tasks. Not automatically remembering that K comes before L in the alphabet without starting at the beginning makes finding one's seat on transport, the theatre, or the cinema time consuming, as is having to rely on iterative addition to work out that seven multiplied by seven equals 49, rather than being able to recall the solution quickly. There can be many 'thingamajigs' or 'whatchamacallits' in the vocabulary of a person who has dyslexia, rather than the actual word for the object being referred to. Although naming ability can relate to expressing words aloud, it also relates to the subvocal. Musicians do not say notes out loud when playing an instrument, but rapid naming has been associated with the sight reading of musical notation, experts in the latter having extremely high rapid-naming ability (Arthur et al., 2021). In addition, when we look at a road sign, we are associating the symbol with a word or activity. Brachacki et al. (1995) found a deficit for knowledge of traffic signs amongst a sample of adults who had dyslexia. This led to the conclusion that the performance of adults with dyslexia was less automatic than that of controls, leading to greater cognitive load, resulting in less spare capacity for recognising road signs.

THE NEUROLOGY OF RAPID NAMING

It has been demonstrated that there is a common neural basis for reading and naming deficits, involving an impairment in integrating phonology and visual images (McCrory et al., 2005). It is central to the asynchrony phenomenon identified as a timing delay (Breznitz, 2008). This asynchrony results in those with dyslexia accessing the image and then the word, a slower process than accessing the word and then the image as is the case for those without dyslexia (Norton et al., 2015). Rapid automatic naming has been partially dissociated from phonological awareness as the skill essential for learning to read, but there is now evidence for a neurobiological distinction between RAN and phonological processing across languages. An MRI study of typical adult readers of Chinese found that phonological decoding ability was related to grey matter volume in the left perisylvian cortex (the area lying around the Sylvian fissure, a deep fissure in each hemisphere that separates the frontal and parietal lobes from the temporal lobe), whereas naming speed was related to volume in a more distributed network across all four lobes (Norton et al., 2015). The rapid naming of letters might access the phonological loop of working memory, but when letters and numbers must be switched quickly, it could involve the central executive and might explain the timing deficit for people with dyslexia in sustaining coordinated orthographic-phonological processing over time (Amtmann et al., 2007).

Brain imaging during phonetic discrimination tasks suggested that the internal accessing of the lexicon was a persistent reading problem observed in dyslexia, and it may derive from inefficient communication within the brain. The combination of fMRI with multi-voxel analysis and functional as well as structural connectivity analysis can be used to disentangle whether phonological deficits are caused by the poor quality of the phonetic representations or difficulties in accessing intact phonetic representations. Boets et al. (2013) found that phonetic representations are hosted in bilateral primary and secondary auditory cortices and that their quality is intact in adults with dyslexia. However, the functional structural connectivity between the bilateral auditory cortices and the left inferior frontal gyrus is significantly hampered in people with dyslexia, suggesting deficient access to otherwise intact phonetic representations.

In general, dysnomia is associated with delayed maturation in the prefrontal cortex, specifically those areas associated with word finding.

SUMMARY

In this chapter we have focused on RAN as an ability separate from phonological processing. The main points were the following.

- Rapid naming has a role in the development of literacy skills.
- Difficulties with rapid naming are one of the most important and persisting cognitive weaknesses amongst individuals with dyslexia.
- The measurement of rapid naming is essential to the diagnosis of dyslexia.
- Weaknesses in rapid naming can affect skills beyond literacy, including verbal communication and the identification of any symbolic material.

6 Making Memory Work

INTRODUCTION

Having identified working memory and rapid naming as significant cognitive weaknesses for people with dyslexia, we now turn to the ways in which these might be addressed. Here we focus on memory strategies, and in Chapter 7 improvements in domains such as literacy and executive functions. As we have demonstrated in Chapters 3 and 4, people with dyslexia have lower working-memory ability, and as a result they will be more susceptible to cognitive overload than others, particularly when presented with verbal and written information. They need help to understand and acknowledge this. All strategies, whether they be for memory, reading, writing, maths, or organisation, should therefore address it. As Levitin (2014) has suggested, if we organise our minds and our lives following the neuroscience of attention and memory, we can all deal with the world in ways that provide the sense of freedom highly successful people enjoy (Levitin, 2014).

COGNITIVE LOAD THEORY

Cognitive load theory was developed in acknowledgement of the limits of working-memory capacity, particularly considering increased demands on adults in educational and workplace settings (Sweller, 1988). The introduction of technology has led to people having to read and process much more text than was anticipated at the beginning of the twenty-first century. It was thought that communication technology would become less text based as it integrated video calling; however, this has not taken place. First, there was the popularity of SMS 'texting' and then instant-messaging tools such as

WhatsApp, both incorporating 'emotion' context communication in icon form (emoticons). The popularity of these means of communication demonstrates that there is a persisting desire to communicate using text, despite the scope for ambiguity and confusion. In addition, the workplace is now replete with emails, open-plan offices, hot desking, along with reductions in administrative support (we are all administrators now). Cognitive load theory has been applied to the development of literacy skills, particularly amongst anglophone students. English is a complex orthographic language because of a lower correspondence between the written form and the phonemes of the language, so it places higher cognitive load when processing text than regular orthographies, which are less dependent on effective cognitive processing (Knight & Galletly, 2020).

Cognitive load has three aspects: *intrinsic*, which is the effort associated with a specific task complexity and the work required to create a permanent state of knowledge; *extraneous*, which are the distractions and unnecessary demands when completing the task; and *germane*, which allows an individual to construct effective and relevant schemata for the task. A fundamental tenet of cognitive load theory is that consideration should be given to the role and limitations of working memory. The demands on each aspect must be minimised so people can process information quicker and learn more effectively. Knowledge of the relationship between working memory and long-term memory can lead to the deliberate development of strategies that address intrinsic overload. Extraneous and germane overload are addressed in Chapter 7.

Throughout life we meet new challenges, and the significance of transitions is referred to in Chapter 9. Suffice it to say here that we all face change, and this requires us to adapt, whether we have dyslexia or not. To do so successfully, everyone has to do the following:

- *Select* areas to concentrate on and choose strategies needed to develop competencies in these. This provides goals, both short term and long term, and allows for the management of personal resources.
- *Optimise* strategies so that one can adapt to challenges and achieve goals.

- *Compensate*: find other ways of dealing with tasks that do not come naturally.

These are things we all must do but they are more important for people with dyslexia, strategy development having been identified as essential to achieving success (Gerber et al., 1992).

BARRIERS TO IMPROVEMENT

There are sometimes barriers to developing strategies, and people with dyslexia need to be open minded so they are not subject to 'proactive inhibition', the process whereby an old way of doing something can prevent us using a new way (Baddeley & Logie, 1999). Old habits die hard, but people with dyslexia need to be open to different approaches. In addition, some people with dyslexia lack confidence, and this can be a major issue. Not being able to forget can be more of a problem than not being able to remember. They cannot forget the embarrassment of situations in which their memory has failed them and the negative experiences at school or in the workplace – for example, having been humiliated for not being able to read aloud fluently, being unable to spell a word correctly when writing on a board, or not being able to calculate solutions to mental arithmetic questions quickly. The fear of public speaking known as *glossophobia*, for example, is often attributed to low self-esteem and the fear of being judged harshly. The philosopher Kierkegaard wrote that 'a person's resiliency can actually be measured by his power to forget' (Hong & Hong, 2000, p. 294), so we sometimes need to put the past behind us. People often have false expectations concerning memory, thinking that they should be able to remember everything, and they often confuse having a good memory with high intelligence. We tend not to have general memory failures but specific temporary failures for some things. There is, therefore, a need for active engagement and reinforcement as information cannot always just be processed once and remembered.

Simple techniques are often the best, but sometimes people are reluctant to rely on them. They may believe these techniques should not be required and might be embarrassed by their need to use them. Generally, it helps if the things we want to remember can be externalised (from our own mind) and made accessible by:

- writing them down;
- making lists;
- using a whiteboard;
- visualising them;
- delegation;
- relying on the functions within a smartphone or computer.

Regarding the last of these, Parker (2022) suggests that by using external entities, 'we create a coupled system in which we delegate part of the task to the technology' and that 'this coupling counts as a cognitive process even though it is not wholly in the head' (p. 150). It reduces the pressure on working-memory capacity and improves functioning by expanding the information storage space available.

Charles Darwin is reported to have written that he followed a golden rule, namely that whenever a published fact, new observation, or thought came across him that was opposed to his general results, he would make a memorandum of it at once without fail, for he had found by experience that such facts and thoughts were far more apt to escape from the memory than favourable ones. The tendency to accept facts and information that support our pre-existing theories and reject information that does not is called confirmation bias.

Simple strategies can reduce cognitive load considerably but should always start with taking control by asking for repetition and seeking clarification. Information is often delivered quickly by those providing it to accommodate their own memory span, and just asking them to slow down will make a difference. 'You did ask me to do A, B, and C?'

DEVELOPING STRATEGIES: PRINCIPLES

There are important principles that underlie the development of strategies, whatever their purpose. It is worth noting here that over the years many interventions have been proposed for addressing the difficulties that derive from having dyslexia. Those that are not evidence based should be ignored, particularly if they include:

- supporting evidence based only on testimonials and anecdotes;
- mention of cures;
- claiming benefits for everyone and anything;
- criticism of evidence-based validated treatments;
- citing limited findings from neurology.

Regarding the last of these, Tallis (2009) recommended that if one comes across something with the preface 'neuro' and it is not directly related to the nervous system itself, it is time to switch on the 'b***s*** detector'.

MEMORY IMPROVEMENT

The starting point is to acknowledge that forgetting falls within Kahneman's 'valley of the normal' (Kahneman et al., 2021). We all find it hard to remember some things at times. Although there are people who seem to have extraordinary memory, often this is just because they have worked very hard on the development of techniques. One example cited in the literature refers to a student at an American university who practised the digit span task (remembering series of numbers) for years. He managed a span of 80 items, but to achieve this he used a grouping and linking strategy combined, relating groups of numbers to the running times of famous athletes. Despite this, his ability to remember series of letters and words was only average. Another individual who had extraordinary memory for numbers, being able to remember 15 presented visually and 63 presented aurally, was below average for remembering pictures (Ericsson & Chase, 1982). Exceptional memory often depends on highly practised strategies. Some people who have spent hundreds of hours developing their memory skills demonstrates this point. For example, Dominic O'Brien, who was once world memory champion, wrote that he devoted six years of his life to achieving this. He suggested that anything you want to remember must be periodically recalled (O'Brien, 1993).

Recall is facilitated by two kinds of access: richness and association (see, for example, Endel Tulving's work, nicely summarised in Tulving, 2001, 2002). Richness refers to the theory that most of the things we have experienced are in long-term episodic memory somewhere. Association means that thoughts can be accessed by semantic memory category names, related words, smells, old songs, or photographs.

All memory techniques involve similar elements based on episodic and semantic memory, including:

- using all the senses;
- visualisation;
- understanding how memory works;
- the use of logic;
- linking and association;
- categorisation;
- repetition.

This focus on different elements of episodic and semantic memory should not be confused with learning styles, a theory that has been discredited over the past decade (Glazzard, 2015).

MEMORY STRATEGIES

As the examples given demonstrate, memory improvement is essentially about strategy development. Having good strategies does not mean having a larger-*capacity* memory, but the best strategies improve the *function* of memory. Evidence for the efficacy of memory training suggests that they are not generally successful across different modalities because improvement tends not to extend beyond the tasks involved in the training programme and improvements do not persist (Melby-Lervåg & Hulme, 2013; Shinaver et al., 2014; Melby-Lervåg et al., 2016). It should be noted that most studies have focused on children and the elderly because they tend to concern education contexts (with children) and neurodegeneration (in the elderly). In the absence of damage to the brain in areas associated with long-term memory, most people do not have trouble storing information they have learned; however, retrieval is not always automatic. In Chapter 4 we referred to long-term memory as being an infinite store, so everything learned is in there somewhere. There are memories within long-term memory that can be relied upon to facilitate recall. To reiterate, these include procedural, episodic, and semantic memories.

Outlined here are the major principles that should be considered. They can all address cognitive load, but the most important are the following.

- Forgetting can be normalised because it is a common human behaviour. It is only when forgetting is excessive that it can be considered a problem. Admitting to having forgotten is less stressful than pretending to have remembered. It is not a reflection of a lack of intelligence. For example, acknowledging that one has left something out while delivering a presentation and offering to 'rewind' is not a crime and reduces anxiety.
- Memory strategies serve different purposes; it is important therefore to ensure that they are task specific. Developing strategies to remember numbers, for example, will not help someone recall names more effectively.
- Good memory strategies need to suit the individual; what works for one person will not always suit another. People need to be open to trying different strategies to find what works best for them.
- The effectiveness of memory strategies can be determined by an individual's knowledge base; this allows for content and context to facilitate recall so we can rely on semantic memory. Memories are more 'sticky' when they can be linked to existing content (in long-term memory). This becomes more important the higher the level of or the more complex the learning being done.
- The best strategies come from an individual's experience, so relying on episodic memory is important.
- Strategies should be simple: people only need the strategies they need; good strategies should rely on as few intellectual processes as necessary. Some are so complex that they just add to cognitive load, so a parsimonious approach is best.
- All of these strategies should, therefore, minimise cognitive load.

TYPES OF STRATEGY

Memory strategies that can help with both storage and retrieval involve similar elements, including repetition, multisensory input, the use of logic and links, relying on imagery and episodic memory, as well as semantic rather than rote memory. The principle of the primacy-recency effect should be acknowledged. This well-established effect states that we are more likely to remember the first (primacy) and last (recency) pieces of information we are given. Therefore, working for short periods of time means we should forget less.

The following types of strategy are commonly used:

- *Meta-memory*, which involves developing an understanding of the nature and limits of memory, as well as considering factors that will facilitate recall. There are many myths and misunderstandings about memory – confusions between short-term memory and working memory, for example. There are differences between storage and retrieval, with individuals not realising the two are related but not the same. There is also a distinction between recognition and recall: the former allows us to rely on visual information, the latter to find the words to describe it. For example, episodic visual memory will help with faces but not names.
- *Categorisation*, which involves linking information into smaller units by association. This is often referred to as *chunking*, which has been strongly related to higher intelligence (Pinker, 2015). It is why tests of reasoning that involve classifying objects and concepts are the best guides to intellectual potential. The key idea is that underlying items are grouped by meaning or structure, so that the category becomes a single structure. As we have noted earlier, short-term memory can only cope with a few items at a time, but chunking allows for more information to be processed there.
- *Elaboration*, which involves assigning meaning to sets of information by using a phrase or sentence, an analogy, or drawing relationships based on specific characteristics. It involves finding additional layers of meaning in new material. It can tap both episodic and semantic memory through the use of metaphors.
- *Transformation*, in which difficult problems are reduced to simpler ones that can be remembered more readily. This approach promotes a deeper understanding, which is a better basis for retrieval.

- *Visualisation* can assist those relying on episodic memory. Past experiences can be visualised and applied to new learning. For example, medical students might rely on previous experience of having conducted a routine procedure.
- *Mnemonic strategies* can improve the recall of information by making it easier to remember, more meaningful, and more concrete by accessing both episodic and semantic memory. They can include acrostics, acronyms, narratives, and rhymes. People who use mnemonics, for example, spend a lot of time building a large collection of chunks that can be stored in and retrieved from long-term memory. Writing about people who have exceptional memory, Groeger (1997) concluded that 'There is very little evidence that exceptional abilities extend beyond the limits of the particular strategies which the mnemonist has learned to use effectively' (p. 242).
- *Using episodic and semantic memory* to create schemas as organisation can make a big difference to memory and recall (Herbert & Burt, 2004). These schemas provide a conceptual structure and context. Self-reference schemata can be particularly effective. The self, being well developed, promotes the elaboration and organisation of information. Self-reference has been described as a uniquely efficient process that 'results in spontaneous, efficient processing of certain kinds of information that people deal with each day – material that is often used, well organised, and exceptionally well elaborated' (Symons & Johnson, 1997, p. 392).

SUMMARY

The focus of this chapter has been on addressing the memory and processing problems associated with dyslexia.

- The emphasis on improvement was through strategy development rather than increasing capacity.
- The importance of addressing cognitive overload has been the dominant theme.
- We have described basic principles underlying the development of good memory techniques.
- It has been noted that memory-training programmes are not effective in improving working-memory capacity.

7 Working Memory and Performance Improvement

INTRODUCTION

Changes in society, with its growing volume of complex texts and instructions, its ever more mind-boggling technology, its simultaneous situations, and its never-ending stream of latest-version software, put increasing pressure on our working memories in our everyday lives (Klingberg, 2009, p. 136).

Kirsh (2000) wrote that 'cognitive overload is a brute fact of modern life. It is not going to disappear. In almost every facet of our work life, and in more and more of our domestic life, the jobs we need to do and the activity spaces in which to perform those jobs are ecologies saturated with overload' (p. 48). Working memory is highly susceptible to overload that occurs when a person encounters more information than the brain can process, so the ability to process information and therefore learn suffers. Trying to process language and comprehending verbal information become more difficult. In general, cognitive overload can have negative effects on task completion (Sweller, 2011).

PERFORMANCE IMPROVEMENT

As a consequence of having a lower working-memory capacity, people with dyslexia will be susceptible to greater cognitive overload than their peers in education and employment. In each of these environments, performance can be enhanced through strategy development, compensation through complementary skills, and accommodations or adjustments. Intrinsic overload can be addressed through developing memory strategies, but also through better studying and working techniques that address germane cognitive overload through the construction of relevant schemata. Consideration of the environment will minimise extraneous overload by controlling factors such as noise and distractions through adjustments.

Individuals should be encouraged to ask three questions:

1. What can I do or what skills can I develop?
2. What else can I do or what alternatives are there?
3. What adjustments or accommodations might make a difference?

This three-strand approach should involve evidence-based decisions made by individuals and those working with and supporting them.

Skill Development

The most effective interventions that address the question 'what can be done about dyslexia?' involve skill development, including complementary skills such as the use of technology, and accommodation or adjustment. These also need to be understood within the context of development across the lifespan, which is an adaptive process and should be both proactive and reactive. That is, individuals can actively effect change but also react to changes such as physical and intellectual maturation, as well as different circumstances. There is a maxim in developmental psychology that states there is no gain without loss and no loss without gain (Baltes, 1987). It is worth reiterating and elaborating here that successful adaptation to developmental changes has been described as involving *selection, optimisation,* and *compensation* (Marsiske et al., 1995; Baltes & Freund, 2003).

Selection refers to the choice of areas for continued development. It can be specialising in a particular academic subject or job, as well as acquiring specific skills that allow one to pursue these. Selection is concerned with both creating and giving direction to development, and managing the fundamental resource limitations inherent in all living systems. It acts to focus development and make the number of challenges and demands facing an individual manageable.

Optimisation reflects the view that development is the internally and externally regulated search for higher levels of functioning, leading to an increase in 'adaptive fitness'. It means that individual competencies are acquired and maintained at desirable levels. Optimisation is aimed at enhancing the strategies used in achieving goals.

Compensation or using complementary skills results from internal and external limits. It relates only to those processes whereby new means are acquired or old means are reconstructed and used to counterbalance functional limits or losses. Compensation is a process by which the impact of internal and external limits is minimised through relying on other means. It is, however, insufficient on its own; just working harder, for example, can lead to negative consequences such as being too exhausted to do anything else (Marsiske et al., 1995).

Skill development is an exercise in selection and optimisation. In the context of someone with dyslexia, it involves setting goals and developing literacy, numeracy, learning, memory, and technological skills to achieve these goals. Skill development is a coordinated activity to achieve a goal in terms of fluency, accuracy, and speed. It involves knowing how to carry out a task, a key aspect being adaptability to new situations and changing task requirements. It is more than just developing skills but includes self-efficacy or the belief an individual holds in their ability. Self-efficacy correlates with the achievements of dyslexic people, influencing 'choice of activity, task perseverance, level of effort expended and ultimately the degree of success achieved' (Klassen, 2002, p. 88).

Compensation/Complementary Skills

There is confusion in the use of the term *compensation* as it is sometimes used in a negative way. Nicolson and Fawcett (1990) referred to people with dyslexia hiding their deficits through conscious compensation, but often it is unconscious. Developing *complementary* skills might be a better description as it reflects a positive and deliberate approach to finding and applying immediate and alternative solutions. The idea of compensation or using complementary means must be conveyed positively to people with dyslexia as it can sometimes be perceived as 'cheating'.

Working harder and investing more time or effort is often regarded as compensation or a complementary skill, but it is a non-cognitive factor related to the individual's personality. Often, people with dyslexia work far too hard because they are reluctant to find other ways of dealing with tasks or simply because this has not occurred to them.

An example of complementary skills development can incorporate the use of technology. For example, according to Lewis (1998), people can:

- augment their strengths so that their abilities counterbalance the effects of any disabilities such as dyslexia.
- provide an alternative mode of performing a task so that the disabilities are compensated for or bypassed entirely.

We can distinguish between 'low-tech' and 'high-tech' aids. The former include relying on the simple techniques described in Chapter 6. High-tech aids include the use of computers and smartphones. Most people now carry around smartphones that have computing power far in excess of that available on the highest-specification desktop computers of a generation ago. This power enables functionality such as text-to-voice readers and dictation software, now superpowered by cloud-based artificial intelligence (AI), which is extremely fast, accurate, and efficient, all within a portable device. The use of computers, voice recognition software, and text-to-speech software all offer more immediate solutions than courses in reading and spelling. Audiobooks, podcasts, and integrated document and text readers are all legitimate means for gaining information. It is not 'cheating' to listen to a recording of a book rather than read it. It in fact reduces cognitive load by removing the need to recognise the words in a text. Now with the advent of large language model (LLM) generative AI chatbots such as ChatGPT (OpenAI), Copilot (Microsoft), Gemini (Google), and Llama (Meta), the speed of information processing, recovery, and production is faster than ever.

Compensation is not a negative process but a deliberate attempt to find ways around problems. Again, it is something that we all do. Wearing reading glasses as one gets older is a technological compensation we now take for granted. Giving dictation and having it transcribed is the most efficient way for some people to deal with written work, whether they have dyslexia or not. This used to be common practice in many offices, before computers became available and people became generalists. Now dictation is possible using software built into most smartphones; however, ten years ago this would have required expensive, specialist software such as Nuance's Dragon Naturally Speaking for common usage.

Accommodations and Adjustments

These involve the adjustments made by others and within the environment in education and employment settings. They include support from colleagues, supervisors, teachers, and tutors, provisions that can be made in situations such as examinations, and adjustments to work tasks and settings. For many people with dyslexia, however, these should only be interim measures. Skills can be improved, and this leads to greater autonomy in learning and work settings. Being flexible about achieving targets in performance appraisals might, for example, allow an individual time to develop new skills or learn how to use a particular piece of software.

SKILL DEVELOPMENT

Overriding all improvement is planning, whether this be for organisation, reading, writing, or daily living. This is the starting point for reducing germane cognitive overload. Further, we need the skills and strategies we need for the common tasks we carry out and so should engage in *satisficing*, a decision-making strategy where we opt for the 'good enough' solution rather than the best solution. This involves a pragmatic effort, because aiming for the optimal solution can be a needless expenditure of time, energy, and resources. The good enough option, rather than the best option, will satisfy the minimum requirements necessary to achieve a particular goal (Levitin, 2014).

Coaching can assist people with dyslexia improve their performance, but this should be context, task, and individual specific, ensuring that the common problems experienced are addressed. Underlying the process, however, should be the development of metacognitive skills – that is, making the unconscious conscious by encouraging people to think more about how they learn and work best, solutions often coming from their own successful experiences. Solutions developed in this way will also provide a greater sense of self-efficacy than if someone is taught or told to do something. It has been argued that coaching can be a disability accommodation (Doyle & McDowall, 2019). It should address the processing problem and cognitive load, as well as allow individuals to utilise their strengths, relying on self-reference and the episodic buffer component of working memory to facilitate recall. The main areas requiring attention are outlined in the following.

Organisation

There is no benefit in not being organised because the cognitive load of tasks becomes considerable. The solution to organisational problems is to work towards being organised; however, this involves setting priorities and targeting easily achievable tasks one at a time.

Procrastination can sometimes be an initiation deficit, so breaking things down into smaller, simpler tasks can help get one started. It is a complex phenomenon with four primary factors: low self-efficacy, low task value, high impulsiveness and distractibility, and a long delay between task onset and completion (Yan & Zhang, 2022). It is not unique to those who have developmental disorders, a cross-cultural study having identified 50 per cent of students and 10–25 per cent of adults who had reported it as something they had experienced (Ferrari & Díaz-Morales, 2007). It has been described as the tendency towards frequent delays in starting or completing tasks that may be present across diverse populations, despite their cultural values.

An alternative approach is called *pre*crastination, that is, the tendency to complete a task early at the expense of extra effort. It has been suggested that some people structure their behaviour this way to free up cognitive resources. This has been referred to as the CLEAR (cognitive-load reduction) hypothesis, that is, the tendency to get things done as soon as possible, and the 'the mere urgency effect', which suggests reducing cognitive demands associated with having to remember what to do when (Rosenbaum et al., 2019; VonderHaar et al., 2019). Some people prefer short deadlines because they avoid the need to monitor the passage of time, which is cognitively taxing, as is the need to rely on prospective memory to remember to do upcoming things (Einstein and McDaniel, 2005; Grondin, 2008). Not only does it free up cognitive resources, it can also lead to the rapid renewal of cognitive resources (Patterson & Kahan, 2020).

In Chapter 4 we referred to the role of the phonological loop component of working memory in time estimation and time management, and the deficit in this is called *dyschronia* (Nicolson & Fawcett, 1995). This concept, more commonly referred to as 'time blindness', has become part of the language of neurodiversity. It is something that can and should be resolved because lateness has implications for the way in which people are perceived professionally, personally, and socially (Rogelberg et al., 2014). The use of time and calendar functions in smartphones can allow one to establish how long a journey or task might take and log reminders of events and when one should leave to be on time. These can be administered using virtual assistants (VAs) on smartphones and are also being significantly enhanced by AI-based chatbots.

Reading Comprehension

The data presented in Chapter 3 suggests that reading speed and comprehension problems persist into adulthood. This is consistent with the findings of studies in which speed has been identified as a major issue, although sometimes this is a deliberate way of addressing the difficulty with comprehension. People with dyslexia over-read and reread, believing that they need to read material several times before understanding or absorbing it. They tend to focus on their difficulties and assume others read and process text perfectly every time. It is possible that this has become a bad habit resulting from failure to gain information in the past, but rereading has been shown to have little or no benefit for improving performance during assessments (Moojen et al., 2020). Nevertheless, studies in which reading rate was controlled for students with dyslexia have shown that they still have more difficulty with literal, inferential, and background questions (Herbert et al., 2004). What is required is focused reading, the use of text structure facilitating comprehension. This begins with an overview, using techniques such as skimming and scanning as well as relying on headings and summaries, then formulating questions and reading just to answer those. Reading examination questions is a an especially important skill in education, particularly given the reason for the referral of many adults. They need to ensure that they are familiar with the subject-specific language of the subject matter as this will enhance understanding (Reis et al., 2020). There is increasing reliance on multiple choice-format tests as an assessment methodology, and these can require specific strategies such as considering alternative responses before reading the question to gain the bigger picture and help focus reading.

Planning Techniques

Written expression for essays and reports places great demands on working memory if it is not done within the implicit and explicit structures of those written forms. Writing is a juggling act that involves vocabulary, grammar, structure, spelling, and punctuation. The way to reduce cognitive load is through planning. One of the generic pieces of advice given to people with dyslexia is to use visual strategies such as mind mapping. These do not work for all, so just listing words or bullet points can help, particularly for letters and emails. Using bullet points or headings for each paragraph of your writing can help reduce the load and assist with focus, and these can be deleted before submission. Formulating questions as a way of planning can be an effective approach to identifying and organising relevant information; it is also necessary for gaining better grades in higher education.

Writing Skills

The purpose of all writing is communication, whether this is educational, work related, or in personal settings. Written information should leave the intended reader better informed, so the author should consider the context of their reader, their level of knowledge about the topic, and the purpose of the writing. Writing should be accessible and understandable, so avoiding overly complex language, using simple words and clear structures, enhances readability, making sure that the writing is not confusing and off-putting.

Spelling

Although spelling is something that has caused adults with dyslexia embarrassment, their skills are often not as bad as they think. Their errors with words are usually close enough for them to use electronic aids, but this is not failsafe. Predictive spelling checkers are prone to anticipation and make errors, 'incontinence' for 'inconsistency' being an example. People can overlearn important job- and course-related words, but also use semantic memory to provide a rationale for technical and irregular words, as well as homophones. Knowing the derivation of words can be particularly helpful.

Proofreading

Checking one's own written work is another activity that places a heavy load on working memory. The simple solution is delegation as another perspective is always helpful. When people read their own work, they anticipate, reading what they think they have written. There are now sophisticated technological solutions to proofreading, whether enhanced grammar checkers or the previously mentioned VAs and AI chatbots.

With all writing tasks, precrastination is to be encouraged. Getting information down first allows time for checking and editing, rather than leaving them to the last minute. When preparing emails, for example, one might draft several and save them for checking later. The further one gets away from a document one has prepared, the more likely it is they will find the errors.

Note Taking/Making Strategies

The cognitive demands of note taking are considerable. It involves listening, identifying important points, processing verbal information, as well as recording these simultaneously. There are multiple cognitive processes that require coordination. A minimalist approach to note taking allows one to focus more on listening, understanding, and interacting. The development of personalised pro formas can be a useful way of identifying and organising relevant information.

Revision Strategies

As with all strategies, those addressing revision should always be task and person specific. Nevertheless, the important principles for revision and test preparation are likely to be the use of imagery – so episodic memory – working for short periods at a time, as well as relying on semantic memory for reasoning and understanding rather than rote memory as much as possible. Revision is something that should be undertaken frequently as this will facilitate recall.

COMPENSATION/COMPLEMENTARY SKILLS

A fundamental tenet of cognitive load theory is that the quality of teaching/learning materials will be improved if consideration is given to the role and limitations of working memory. Solutions to some difficulties lie in the efficient use of technological aids as these can both reduce cognitive load as well as make storage in memory more effective. They need to be practical in terms of their application but can include the following.

Text-to-Speech Software and Audiobooks

These provide an alternative to reading and can be particularly effective as they bypass the need to recognise words so reduce cognitive load. They can also provide the context, which enhances comprehension.

Web-Based Materials

The way in which information is presented is an important factor in addressing cognitive load. Again, visually presented information minimises the demands on reading and can be very powerful, but the design should be considered carefully.

Planning Software

This can be helpful in organising thoughts and ideas, as well providing a memory aid.

Timers

As we have seen, time estimation can be undermined by problems with working memory. Estimates can be made a reality by working to a clock or electronic device.

Voice Recognition Software

The individuals described in Chapter 3 have more than competent verbal ability. The quickest way for them to achieve a match between this and their written work would be through dictation. Often, people with dyslexia have found it difficult to dictate in a traditional way as they can't remember what they have said. The advantage of voice recognition software is that they can easily refer to previous sections. It is not perfect and best considered as a tool for getting words on the page quickly.

Grammar and Spelling Checkers

These are now standard in computer software used for producing written documents. Care is needed as they are never failsafe.

Sometimes it can be difficult to convince people to rely on technology. They believe it is 'cheating' to listen rather than read, but people with visual impairments 'read by listening'. Because of the difficulties they experience with information processing, they may have developed a dislike for technology that, historically, may have required significant training to use effectively.

In terms of cognitive load theory, however, there are important considerations concerning the use of technology, particularly the internet and portable cloud-based applications. Designers of technological solutions need to be aware that reading comprehension declines as the number of links increases. Readers must devote more attention and intellectual effort to evaluating the links and deciding whether to click on them, leaving less attention and fewer cognitive resources to devote to understanding. Interactive websites and reading online can be sources of overload. There is a strong correlation between the number of links in an online source and cognitive overload, thereby affecting the reading comprehension of online readers (Carr, 2020).

ADJUSTMENTS AND ACCOMMODATIONS

In the United Kingdom context, dyslexia can be considered a disability for the purposes of the Equality Act 2010, and in the United States with reference to the Americans with Disabilities Act of 1990. It must be demonstrated that dyslexia has a significant impact on the person's day-to-day activities. If the effects of dyslexia have a substantial impact on the latter, organisations can be expected to make reasonable adjustments or accommodations, the underlying philosophy being inclusion. Unfortunately, 'reasonable adjustment' is a compound noun that often leads to a one-size-fits-all approach. It would be better if we were to think about 'adjustments that are reasonable'. It is always a matter to be considered carefully, but there are certain fundamental principles that underlie the making of adjustments. They should:

- be evidence based – relying on the results of research and formal assessment not self-identification;
- lead to inclusion rather than exclusion – too many adjustments can result in the latter;
- not compromise the requirements of a training course or job – having the competencies to undertake either is fundamental;
- not place overwhelming administrative or financial demands on institutions and organisations.

There is a point at which adjustments can become unreasonable. This can lead to perceptions of unfairness and result in conflict. For example, it is not reasonable for every dyslexic person to be assigned a full-time reader and scribe in the workplace, whereas this may be appropriate for a university examination.

Time Adjustments

Speed of reading and writing has been found to be the most persisting literacy difficulty for people with dyslexia (Reis et al., 2020). People with dyslexia need to work harder at tasks others can take for granted; their intrinsic cognitive load is greater. In general, therefore, the most important adjustment for any individual is time. Developing new skills involves unlearning old ways of completing tasks, developing different approaches, and consolidating these. Expectations regarding the times at which people meet performance targets and assignment deadlines should be modified, especially when there has been a late diagnosis.

Candidates should be allowed extra time to complete formal examinations. This will not give them extra knowledge but address skill deficits such as lack of fluent comprehension, and there is ample evidence to support this. It also allows for careful planning and proof-reading. There is a standard figure of 25 per cent, but this is a convention rather than evidence based. It is enough for some but not all. The best basis for determining a time allowance at a behavioural level is speed of working (reading and writing). The amount of time that is allowed can be based on the discrepancy between the expected rate and the speed at which the individual reads and writes. Someone who reads at half speed might be allowed 50 per cent extra time, although it has been suggested that this might be advantageous rather than equalising. Sometimes people 'want extra time to provide a safety net that relieves their anxiety about running out of time' (Harrison et al., 2022, p. 306). Nevertheless, too much extra time might lead to fatigue and be counterproductive. Common sense should prevail, and the candidate should be consulted in deciding what might be considered reasonable for them.

Allowing candidates who read slowly to have extra time to mitigate their difficulty should be obvious, but there are other situations in which this might be appropriate. As we have described in Chapter 5, rapid naming is one of the more persistent processing problems associated with dyslexia. This can have an impact on word finding. When undergoing verbal tests, therefore, allowing candidates to seek repetition and clarification, as well as giving them more time to respond, would be reasonable.

What does seem to be an increasing problem for people with dyslexia is the presentation of tests via technology. Computer-based testing can lead to faster scoring, more precise and accurate measurement, and can facilitate learning by the provision of feedback (Pengelley et al., 2025). However, there is an assumption that computer-based and paper-based tests are equivalent because they use the same content (questions). However, based on systematic research, it has been argued that it is difficult to attain equivalence between computer and paper presentation, and that this is probably impossible to achieve. Further, some studies have shown that comprehension, retention, and attention are better when information is presented on paper rather than on a computer screen. There does not appear to be any significant difference between those who have grown up with computers (digital natives) and those who have not (digital migrants). Regarding dyslexic candidates, it has been suggested that screen-based material places increased demands on cognitive processing, especially on individual working-memory capacity, and changes the metacognitive strategies they engage in to approach tasks, so people who have low working-memory capacity are disadvantaged (Pengelley et al., 2025). For example, it may not be possible to annotate an online test. An important issue is how readily individuals are able to gain an overview of what is in front of them. Paper-based tests allow immediate access to the text in its entirety. As a general rule, it is easier to look through items and move backwards and forwards when using paper. Individual trainees have also commented on the fact that computer-based tests do not allow them to use the strategies they have developed over the years. The paratextual information such as page turning, relying on page numbers, and being able to 'refer back' are important. Computer-based testing has cost advantages and is 'greener', but offering a choice between completing paper- or computer-based tests could be considered a reasonable adjustment, and administrative expedience might not be sufficient justification for not doing so.

Other considerations when adjusting for candidates with dyslexia in examinations relate to the timing of tests and the environment in which they are completed. There will always be individual differences, but if people with dyslexia are prone to cognitive overload, the timetabling of sessions should be considered as they are unlikely to be at their best later in the day. In addition, maintaining effort over a lengthy period can exacerbate overload, which might be mitigated by being able to take breaks during examinations. They can also be more susceptible to distractions because of the impact of their processing weaknesses on executive functions, and some try to enhance reading comprehension by vocalising when reading. Both matters can be addressed by providing candidates with a room separate from other candidates.

The Environment

Extraneous cognitive overload can be addressed in educational and work settings by considering environmental factors. Many office environments are not ideal for people with dyslexia: hot desking does not help with organisation and memory; open plan offices are replete with distractions and interruptions. The adjustments that might be made should be clear, as both can be avoided. Nevertheless, sometimes the obvious can be counterproductive. Working from home at least for some of the time has become common practice, particularly in the post-Covid era. However, while this might allow someone to structure their day and environment to meet their needs, it is not necessarily effective. If people with complementary knowledge are in easy earshot or eyeshot from each other, the result is usually that they consult and help each other. They may also interrupt each other too, so the resulting social and work ecology is not unambiguously for the better for everyone. Nevertheless, in teams of people, cognitive effort can be distributed, thereby reducing individual stress (Kirsh, 2000).

SUMMARY

This chapter has focused on performance improvement, again placing it within the context of cognitive overload. We have:

- explained performance improvement in terms of selection, optimisation, and compensation;
- outlined some of the specific strategies that can reduce cognitive overload and address the ongoing literacy and organisational difficulties experienced by individuals with dyslexia;
- suggested alternative means, including the use of technology;
- addressed the adjustments that can be made to support individuals in academic and workplace settings.

8 Working Memory and Counselling

INTRODUCTION

Confidence comes from feeling competent, so there should be automatic gains as performance improves. Nevertheless, the impact of non-cognitive factors can be entrenched and pervasive, so there is sometimes a need for counselling (McLoughlin & Leather, 2013). When adults have been identified as having dyslexia, they begin to realise why they have faced challenges in life and start to understand themselves better. Some will feel that they can unburden themselves and talk about matters beyond the reasons that prompted them to seek a diagnosis. The cognitive profiles outlined in Chapter 3 do not indicate how a person *experiences* dyslexia; however, the approaches outlined in this chapter do help us with understanding how people's experiences can influence their functioning. To this end, coaches, psychologists, and trainers do not need to become therapists, but it can be helpful for them to understand and adopt some of the fundamental principles and practices of formal counselling.

GENERAL AND SPECIALIST COUNSELLING

Miles et al. (1998) drew a distinction between generalist and specialist counselling expertise. The former was described as being common to all forms of counselling, such as being a good listener, showing empathy, and being non-judgemental. The latter involves having a 'technical knowledge over and above their ability to listen and discuss' (Miles et al., 1998, p. 103).

Professional counsellors working with people with dyslexia need to understand the nature of the syndrome, as well as its manifestations and consequences, particularly how it might impact on information processing and verbal communication. Without this, interpretations and interventions can be inappropriate. Counsellors do not need to be experts in dyslexia, but it is necessary to recognise that someone who has dyslexia will have a fundamental difference in their cognition that makes certain tasks more difficult for them compared to others. They must be aware of how these difficulties have operated to produce further complications in a person's life and behaviour. The relationship between behavioural and cognitive difficulties should be acknowledged and understood, including knowing that every experience, positive and negative, may be stored in long-term memory. Counsellors need to adapt their approach to consider the unique processing style of their clients. They need to be aware of the risk of cognitive overload as this can lead to confusion. Clients with dyslexia might find it hard to understand key concepts, have trouble remembering the details of a session, and feel overwhelmed, which can lead to feelings of anxiety and disengagement. Overload can be addressed by:

- providing written materials;
- repeating new concepts;
- reviewing previous sessions;
- adapting the communication style to one that suits the individual;
- establishing realistic goals and expectations;
- relying on technology to help with retention and recall.

Essentially, it should be ensured that the client is not overwhelmed as this will affect comprehension and retention, thus undermining the counselling process.

COUNSELLING AIMS AND ISSUES: GOAL SETTING

The aims of counselling are to:

- enhance self-confidence;
- enable someone to live, study, and work in a more satisfying, resourceful way;
- promote general wellbeing.

Counselling should be an extension of the assessment process, developing self-understanding, including:

- explaining what dyslexia is and how it affects people;
- 'normalising' characteristics;
- helping to establish long- and short-term goals;
- advising on strategies and sources of help;
- assisting with the process of reframing.

Another function of counselling can be to address non-cognitive factors, including:

- stress and anxiety;
- low self-esteem and feelings of incompetence;
- a feeling of loss over what might have been;
- helplessness, resulting from a limited understanding of learning abilities and disabilities.

To some extent these are addressed by dealing with the behavioural characteristics. Improved skills and performance, greater self-understanding and self-efficacy, or feeling more in control can diminish anxiety. In a study of medical students, for example, confidence in their capabilities and their knowledge of the content correlated with performance in verbal tests, self-confidence protecting them from the negative effects of stress and anxiety (Ferreira et al., 2020).

There are many theoretical approaches to counselling, and most might have something to offer. Nevertheless, reviews of the outcomes of different models have led to the conclusion that there is little evidence to show that one approach is necessarily better than another, non-specific factors such as the relationship between client and counsellor being more important. The difference in outcomes appears to be contingent on the effectiveness of the therapist rather than the theoretical model they rely on (Roth et al., 1996; Wampold, 2013). Here we focus on the work of Beck (2020), who considered that treatments for conditions such as anxiety and depression focus too much on past events rather than current beliefs. His work has its roots in that of

Ellis (1962), whose rational emotive behaviour therapy (RET) was one of the main pillars of Beck's cognitive-behavioural therapy (CBT).

BASIC COUNSELLING PRINCIPLES

Counselling has been defined by stipulating the central qualities of good helping relationships, which are both *necessary* in that change will not occur if they are not present, and *sufficient* in that, if they exist, change will occur (Rogers, 1951). What have been defined as the core conditions are the following.

Cognitive Empathy

This entails seeing the world of another from their point of view, that is, 'standing in someone else's shoes'. This involves:

- listening actively and sensitively;
- trying to make sense of what is heard;
- understanding the other person in their own terms;
- checking to ensure the meaning has been interpreted properly.

Non-judgemental Acceptance

This is described as 'unconditional positive regard' and involves accepting the other person as being a worthwhile human being, regardless of their faults and failings.

Genuineness

This involves the helper being open to their own feelings, being fallible, vulnerable, and imperfect, not knowing all the answers. It is also known as congruence.

THEORETICAL APPROACHES

Contrary to the social model of disability, which places responsibility on society to accommodate the needs of people who have developmental disorders such as dyslexia, research has demonstrated the importance of the individual acting with agency. One of the factors that has been identified as crucial to the success of individuals is the process of reframing or redeployment, involving several stages (Gerber et al., 1996):

- recognition that one has a learning disorder;
- understanding the nature and implications of dyslexia for the individual;
- acceptance that there are issues to be dealt with;
- planning what action to take to achieve short- and long-term goals.

Cognitive restructuring approaches to counselling can be effective in the reframing process. Rational emotive therapy (RET), developed by Ellis (1962), for example, assumes that maladaptive feelings are caused by irrational beliefs. The theory behind it is that it is not events that directly cause emotions and behaviours and determine reactions, but one's beliefs about the events. It distinguishes between rational and irrational beliefs and suggests that people can react to situations in healthy or unhealthy ways. The goal of the therapy is to promote *unconditional self-acceptance.* He proposed that it is possible for people to accept themselves as they are, suggesting that the actions of an individual can be a source of validation but should not determine their worth. Ellis (1962) argues that through mistaken assumptions, people place excessive demands upon themselves, proposing an ABC model in which A is Activating events, B is Beliefs and interpretations, and C is Consequences of behaviours. Counselling involves challenging B, described as irrational beliefs held in long-term memory, and replacing them with rational beliefs. The latter are defined as being flexible, non-extreme, and logical. In contrast, irrational beliefs are rigid, extreme, and illogical or inconsistent with reality. There are four types of irrational belief:

- demandingness – 'if my report was good my boss would have complimented me';
- awfulising – 'if I fail this examination my career is over';
- low frustration tolerance – 'I won't volunteer as I can't do a good job';
- depreciation – 'I burnt the dinner – I make a mess of everything'.

Changing beliefs involves a disputation process in which the client is asked to consider whether there is any evidence for their current beliefs, whether they are consistent with reality, and whether they are helpful. Not being able to forget stressful episodes is often more difficult than not being able to remember, and people are prone to negativity bias. We give more weight and attention to negative things than we do to positive things (Rozin & Royzman, 2001), and the role of the hedonic detector in working memory plays a part in this. Effectively, people are encouraged to rely on semantic rather than episodic memory to change their beliefs.

Rational emotive therapy (RET) was the forerunner to the CBT developed by Beck (2020). It has been intensively researched, and findings indicate that this type of therapy has been one of the most effective treatments, particularly for anxiety and depression. No other form of psychotherapy has more support from research and studies to validate its fundamental constructs. It is particularly appropriate for people who have learning disorders as it can be integrated into an information-processing paradigm, the focus being on changing patterns of thinking (David et al., 2018).

CBT considers psychological problems to be the result of the negative ways in which individuals think about themselves. It is based in attribution theory, in which behaviour is thought to be determined by the causes an individual associates with it. Attributions are made to either internal causes that are self-blaming or external causes such as circumstances. An example of someone with dyslexia making an internal attribution would be for them to blame their literacy difficulty on lack of intelligence; an external attribution would be for them to blame it on poor schooling. The former would also be regarded as stable, implying that it can't be changed. The latter would be considered unstable as something can be done to make up for poor educational opportunities. Attributions can also be global, that is, associated with many aspects of life, such as dealing with any kind of paperwork, or specific, where difficulties with written work are blamed on a particular problem with spelling.

Individuals who are inclined towards giving global, stable, and internal explanations for negative events are vulnerable to depression. When things do not go well, they think badly of themselves, and their confidence and self-esteem are affected. In contrast, people who have good mental health respond to positive events by making internal, stable, and global attributions, and when things do not go well, external, unstable, and specific attributions. As we suggested earlier, because of their inefficient working-memory system, people with dyslexia might be more susceptible to making internal, self-blaming attributions. These will influence their self-perception, expectations concerning the outcome of future events, and feelings about the ability to influence these events as well as their motivation to do so. As we have written in Chapter 4, every experience we have is retained in long-term memory – the good, the bad, and the ugly. Consistent with negativity bias, the hedonic detector will veer more towards the latter, so counselling might focus on helping people to move towards the neutral point on the valence scale.

Cognitive-behavioural therapy (CBT) involves questioning and collaborating with clients so that they can discover for themselves the distortions in their thinking, that is, their inappropriate attributes, and can then make changes that are consistent with reality. It focuses on changing people's thinking. We are volitional beings, so the choice to act is ours, and our sense of purpose is defined by reaching for the upper limits of our natural abilities and learned skills, and by facing challenges with courage and conviction (Shermer, 2018, p. 251). Positive outcomes have been reported for the treatment of anxiety and depression, as well as improving self-esteem and motivation (David et al., 2018). A fundamental tenet of CBT is that anxiety comes from the appraisal of situations, not the event itself. That is, there is a trigger event and a negative appraisal of it, leading to anxious feelings, so the way people think affects the way they feel. Again, according to Baddeley's account of working memory (Baddeley et al., 2012), the hedonic detector is more likely to access negative experiences when working memory is inefficient.

A cognitive-behavioural approach attempts to identify the typical distorted cognitive processes of individuals. Writing specifically about counselling and dyslexia, Scott (2004, cited in McLoughlin & Leather, 2013) included the following.

- Dysfunctional schemas – general beliefs that are at the back of our minds that provide reference points for choices in our life: 'I am lazy; I would do better if I worked harder – it is what teachers told me at school.' These become ingrained beliefs.
- Cognitive distortions – biased interpretations of external events that lead us to catastrophise: 'My boss found errors in my work and that I am slow with my work; he thinks I am stupid.'
- Overgeneralisations – taking one event as representative of all others: 'I made a spelling mistake; my spelling is terrible'; 'The presentation didn't go well – I am really bad at it.'
- Making internal attributions – attributing to oneself unwarranted responsibility for all negative events: 'The project wasn't a success, so it must be my fault.'

By addressing such distortions, people with dyslexia can be helped to reframe and move on to find solutions.

This approach to counselling involves questioning clients so that they can discover for themselves the distortions in their thinking and can then make changes that are consistent with reality. Scott and Snowling (2004) recommends CBT as the most powerful and long-term solution to problems with anxiety. They suggest that some of the negative thoughts and beliefs particularly common amongst people with dyslexia are (p. 269):

- oil stick thoughts – transferring negative feelings about one aspect of one's life to every aspect: 'I forget things so I must be stupid';
- the habit of beating oneself up – self-blaming for causing others inconvenience: 'I am always late'; 'I have to ask others to check my work, so I am a nuisance';
- giving power away to other people – that is, learned helplessness: 'My wife deals with all the domestic paperwork and won't let me do it';
- old behaviour that gets in the way – unlearning bad habits can be harder that developing new skills: 'I have to reread everything before I remember it';

- separating the truth from the lie – thinking problems are much worse than they really are: 'I can't read aloud'; 'My spelling is dreadful.'

CBT is transdiagnostic as it can be applied to several mental health conditions. Likewise, acceptance and commitment therapy (ACT), developed by Hayes et al. (2011), provides what has been described as a third-wave cognitive-behavioural approach to counselling. It is empirically based and belongs to the positive psychology movement. Acceptance and commitment therapy (ACT) has been applied to physical and cognitive conditions. The emphasis is on acknowledging that many of the negative experiences people endure are inevitable features of human life, the goal of therapy being to encourage acceptance of this and flexibility in how people respond to challenges. Attempts to eliminate or supress undesirable experiences are discouraged, and strategies for addressing stigma and misunderstanding are taught. Clarifying goals and strategy development for their achievement are emphasised. There does not appear to be much in the way of research directed towards the effectiveness of ACT when working with individuals with dyslexia, but its application is being encouraged within the neurodiversity movement.

NON-COGNITIVE ISSUES

Clark and Beck (2010) provided a modified cognitive neurophysiological model of Beck's cognitive formulation of anxiety and depression. This incorporated an account of the cognitive and neural mediation processes of cognitive therapy. Empirical evidence suggested that the effectiveness of cognitive therapy could be associated with reduced activation of subcortical regions implicated in the generation of negative emotion, and increased activation of higher-order frontal regions involved in cognitive control of negative emotions. Stress and anxiety are factors that can undermine the ability to function effectively in learning and work situations, exacerbating behavioural difficulties (Schweizer et al., 2019). They can have a particular impact on cognition, including working memory (Sandi, 2013; Moran, 2016). It can therefore be beneficial for people to learn relaxation techniques. These are well documented and include the following:

- visualisation – producing feelings of calm and wellbeing by training people to use pictures in their minds of themselves in safe, warm, and comforting environments;
- deep breathing – which stimulates relaxation and reduces stress and anxiety;
- progressive relaxation – focusing on the major muscle groups of the body, group by group;
- reinterpretation – such as cognitive reappraisal so that anxiety is seen as excitement.

Mindfulness is deserving of particular attention as some systematic studies have addressed its potential impact on learning generally, working memory, and dyslexia. It is incorporated into ACT therapy. Vorontsova-Wenger et al. (2022) reported that short mindfulness programmes had a beneficial effect on the cognition and academic performance of undergraduates. Likewise, Jankowski and Holas (2020) reported positive effects for the general efficiency of cognitive processes amongst a student population. Regarding dyslexia, Tarrasch et al. (2016) concluded that 'mindfulness-based interventions can contribute to improvements in reading as well as the quality of life of individuals with dyslexia' (p. 14). Reporting the findings of a mindfulness for study course, Krcmar and Horsman (2014) cited student participants as saying that they felt able to approach their work in a calmer, less stressed, and more productive way.

None of these will remove anxiety, especially if its source remains constant. If having to deal with an overbearing manager or a demanding course is the cause, this will not be resolved just through stress management, but the symptoms can be controlled. Negative emotions influence processes in attention and working memory, so when people are less anxious, there should be an improvement in performance (Lisica et al., 2022).

REFERRING ON

One of the characteristics of a mature professional is knowing when they are out of their depth and other expertise is required. Professionals working closely with people with dyslexia need to be aware of the possibility of their clients becoming more dependent rather than independent. There are people with dyslexia whose life experiences have been such that they need in-depth counselling. Further, as suggested in Chapter 4 and according to the Baddeley model of working memory, people with dyslexia can be prone to depression, and sometimes this requires more than a talking therapy.

SUMMARY

In this chapter we have addressed counselling that might be appropriate for individuals with dyslexia.

- The emphasis has been on developing self-understanding so that individuals can reframe their learning disorder.
- We have addressed non-cognitive factors such as confidence, low self-esteem, stress, and anxiety.
- We have described cognitive-based therapies such as RET, CBT, and ACT as the most appropriate models, based on an understanding of working memory.
- There has also been reference to the ways in which individuals can manage stress and anxiety.

9 Working Memory and Career Development

INTRODUCTION

The provision of suitable career counselling for people who have developmental learning disorders such as dyslexia can be one of the most important areas of professional work; however, this provision is generally under-resourced. Appropriate guidance, especially at times of transition, can assist a person to find their niche in life. There are unique challenges for those advising people with dyslexia. Unless the potential barriers presented by a learning disorder and the ways in which these might be overcome are understood, people will be unable to make informed career choices. They need to know that dyslexia is an information-processing problem, notably in working memory, and what the implications can be for their future employment and education. It might limit the range of career options open to someone, so being familiar with the nature of learning disorders and understanding the content of reports from diagnostic assessments, as well as a knowledge of strategies and adjustments that can help people function, will be important.

Over the years, we have met people with dyslexia working in most occupations and at all levels. Having the syndrome is not an insurmountable barrier to success in educational and work settings. We have seen that dyslexia will never be the only thing to limit someone's success. People who have neurodevelopmental disorders do not constitute a homogenous population. They will not, therefore, benefit from a 'one-size-fits-all' approach to career development, particularly if this is based on myths about their talents and abilities. It is a mistake to guide individuals into careers and job roles based on assumptions and misinformation.

MYTHS AND MISGUIDANCE

Individuals with dyslexia are prone to *stereotype threat*, which occurs when there is the pressure of being judged based on stereotyped group membership (Steele & Aronson, 1995). Expectations are lower, and this can lead to underperformance, especially in test settings (Piotrowska & Barratt, 2024). Equally, positive stereotypes that focus on gifts that create an advantage can raise false expectations. Odegard and Dye (2024) have argued that this can inadvertently stigmatise and isolate those who do not meet the positive stereotype. An important issue in goal setting is ensuring that people with dyslexia do not fall for myths about the disorder, such as assuming that they will have strong visual abilities and should therefore enter artistic endeavours or work with computers. Falsified notions, such as learning styles, persist regardless of the education and training professionals undertake (Macdonald et al., 2017). Although it has been suggested that the neurological organisation of their brains leads to people with dyslexia having stronger functioning in some areas, much of the evidence for this is based on anecdote, as well as speculation about creative and gifted people, many living and some deceased. There are living actors, writers, and artists who have been identified as having dyslexia, and there are disproportionate numbers of students with dyslexia attending art colleges (Wolff & Lundberg, 2002). It has also been suggested that there are many entrepreneurs with dyslexia (Logan, 2009). Whether this reflects innate abilities or a reaction to experience is open to question, and there is a false logic in assuming that the success of scientists, artists, architects, and entrepreneurs is attributable to them having dyslexia or any other conditions. Studies of successful entrepreneurs, for example, have identified factors such as a high need for achievement, a strong inner locus of control, and an ability to delegate (Rauch & Frese, 2000; Logan, 2009).

There are systematic studies that have explored the notion that dyslexic people have visual strengths, but these have 'met with limited success' (Alexander-Passe, 2010, p. 3) and the results have often been contradictory. The notion that people with dyslexia possess unique strengths rather than produce difficulties is often based on the simplistic views of the functioning human brain, promoting neuro-myths such as left brain/right brain and differences in learning styles. As we have written in Chapter 2, the efficiency of the brain is determined by connectivity, so to focus on interactions in one or more specific regions or divisions between left and right hemisphere functions is naïve to say the least. There are an increasing number of studies that employ fMRI scans, but these are largely inconclusive. Besides, as Russell (2020) points out, 'not many diagnoses involve brain scans, so the neurological differences of neurodivergent people are not seen but inferred' (p. 291). The prefix 'neuro-' often provides a credibility that is undeserved (Weisberg et al., 2008), particularly as, overall, 'studies have failed to demonstrate that people who have dyslexia are more creative than ordinary people' (Stein, 2023, p. 8).

In a report prepared by the Dyslexia Foundation (Gilger, 2017), most of the studies that consider the 'special talents' of individuals with dyslexia were reviewed. The major conclusion of this review was that notions regarding giftedness and dyslexia are not evidence based, and there are no clear links between the two. They addressed two main claims about dyslexia:

1. It is associated with entrepreneurial success and creativity.
2. It is correlated with specialised skills in the domain of visual processing.

They concluded that:

> if career differences exist, there is currently no evidence that such differences are due to specific inherent talents or better than average skills that suit one or the other of these career types, nor is it currently possible to determine whether success in these careers is due to inherent strengths that fit such careers, or because these careers are chosen by default in order to avoid careers requiring extensive reading.
>
> (p. 112)

There are two hypotheses derived from this:

1. The early choice hypothesis, which implies that adolescents and adults seek opportunities that focus on strengths and make career choices that do not place a heavy demand on academic skills, suggesting a need for good career counselling. In the United Kingdom, at around 16 years of age, students can choose between academic examination-based courses and those that are vocational and coursework evaluated. People who find academic courses difficult because of the literacy and memory demands, not because they lack intelligence, take the latter route so are able to focus on their competencies and be assessed on their strengths.
2. The compensatory coping mechanisms hypothesis, which proposes that individuals with dyslexia develop unconventional coping mechanisms and modes of thinking in adolescence and adulthood. They are used to finding their own and often alternative ways of learning and working, so become adept at thinking laterally out of necessity.

Transitions

We have been asked whether we conduct assessments for 'stealth dyslexia', a reference to an analogy someone has used to refer to the late onset of the behavioural characteristics of dyslexia. The processing problems associated with dyslexia will have always been there but may have been masked by the need to cope with constantly increasing demands. One of the reasons for suggesting that a good theoretical model should enable someone to predict what might be challenging in the future is that everyone faces a series of transitions – life changes to which we must adjust. The transition individuals face when moving from school to work is one that educationalists recognise, but there is not enough acknowledgement of how demanding this can be for those who have developmental learning disorders (McLoughlin, 2018). An understanding of the limitations of working-memory capacity allows us to make sense of the challenges people face from reading accuracy to fluency, fluency to generalisation, and generalisation to adaptation (Peavler, 2024). If they lack prerequisite skills and there are gaps in their knowledge, working memory can easily become overloaded, meaning that they do not have the automaticity needed for new learning.

It has been suggested that we need to understand transitions within the context of the lifespan, particularly as career progression has become more fragmented, with multiple careers not being unusual now. This would seem particularly relevant to people with dyslexia, as some do not follow the *typical* paths, their development being less linear than it is for others. In the workplace the demands on independent learning skills, self-confidence, and the ability to absorb new information, understand job tasks, comprehend work culture, and follow procedures are considerable. In the twenty-first century dealing with constant change is a key aspect of any occupation: in-service training, job redefinition, promotion to higher levels of a job, moving from one department to another, from job to job, from employment back to unemployment. Developments in technology have provided individuals who have literacy difficulties with solutions. At the same time, they have presented problems, and the rate of change can be overwhelming. Developments in technology have also placed greater demands on literacy, any computing task requiring some reading skills, and according to cognitive load theory possibly ones that are different from those needed when reading from the printed page. Change can be challenging and demands psychological energy that enables coping and adaptation. It can also prove to be stressful, leading to anxiety, thereby exacerbating the processing difficulties associated with dyslexia.

As we have written earlier, a good model of dyslexia should allow people to predict what might be difficult in the future, so assisting individuals to cope with demands at any one stage is not enough. People with dyslexia may not have developed the skills they need to affect a positive adaptation, and often these do not develop automatically. Smith-Spark and Fisk (2007) point out that working-memory deficits can have 'a significant impact on planning, problem solving, acting under novel situations, and learning. Relevant support must, therefore, be provided across a range of modalities for adults with dyslexia to achieve their full potential in both educational and employment settings' (p. 51). It is often at times of transition, because of having been successful, that many individuals with dyslexia seek an explanation for the problems they face and present for an initial diagnostic assessment, as well as ask for help with their skills. Promotion, for example, can place increased demands on organisational and social skills, as well as written-language tasks such as report writing. Even adults with dyslexia but who have done well academically and professionally think their dyslexia has become worse. It has probably not; they are just facing increasingly complex tasks in their work and social lives (Price & Patton, 2002; Gerber & Price, 2003).

ISSUES IN CAREER GUIDANCE

An idiographic approach to career counselling is required. This should be based on knowledge of abilities and potential barriers, but be one that develops an understanding of these and how they might be overcome, thereby enabling individuals to make informed choices. They need a good understanding of themselves, their abilities, and their skills, knowing how to match these to job demands. Specialist career guidance for individuals with dyslexia, or any other learning disorder, is not generally available. Nevertheless, those who find themselves in a position in which they need to advise students and adults should develop their knowledge of the impact syndromes might have, based on evidence not myths and stereotypes. Without acknowledging and understanding the limitations placed upon people by their learning disorder, career guidance can prove unhelpful. We have argued in this book that, based on a working-memory model, we are referring to a syndrome that has an impact on verbal as well as written communication, organisation, time management, planning, and adaptation to change. These are all domains that need to be understood and addressed if individuals are to be successful in life and employment. The most effective approach is based on a decision-making model (see, for example, McLoughlin et al., 1994; McLoughlin & Leather, 2013).

SUCCESSFUL ADJUSTMENT

Most of the research in the field of dyslexia has adopted a deficit model devoted to identifying the factors that make life harder for people who have developmental disorders, but to understand those that have been successful, researchers have adopted a 'risk and resilience' framework. As we have outlined in Chapter 2, having dyslexia can be a risk factor, that is, something that might impact negatively on an individual's life, leading to failure in academic and employment settings. Resilience refers to 'a class of phenomena characterised by good outcomes despite serious threats to adaptation or development' (Masten, 2001, p. 228), although failure does not always have negative consequences and can sometimes be motivating (Tanner, 2009). In our own research in which we surveyed graduates who had been provided with adjustments during their university courses, persistence and determination were commonly identified as things that had enabled them to achieve (Martin & McLoughlin, 2012).

Gregg (2014) summarised the findings of research into resilience by writing that successful adults who have neurodevelopmental disorders 'adapt to life events through self-awareness and acceptance of their disability, are proactive and persevere, and are emotionally stable and able to tolerate stress. They are goal directed and can establish and use effective support systems' (p. 87). She identified the last of these as being fundamental to the maintenance of motivation and perseverance. Likewise, Nalavany et al. (2011) identified several factors, including organisation and the role of good support systems. Family support in particular buffers, mitigates, and protects the effects of negative emotional experiences (Carawan et al., 2016). The results of these studies are consistent with those of Goldberg et al. (2003), who carried out a longitudinal study and identified through six attributes common to adults with developmental learning disorders who experience a successful adult life:

1. self-awareness: understanding one's strengths and weaknesses and recognising how the learning disability affects different aspects of their life;

2. proactivity: taking initiative and actively engaging in shaping their future, rather than passively accepting circumstances;
3. perseverance: demonstrating resilience and adaptability, learning from setbacks, and finding alternative paths to success;
4. goal setting: establishing clear, realistic, and attainable goals across multiple domains of life;
5. effective use of social support systems: seeking and maintaining relationships with mentors, family, and peers who provide guidance and encouragement;
6. emotional stability and coping strategies: developing strategies to manage stress, frustration, and emotional challenges associated with learning difficulties.

Self-awareness, perseverance, goal setting, strategy development, and supportive relationships are common to all the studies that have considered the success of people with dyslexia (Gerber et al., 1992; Spekman et al., 1992; Carawan et al., 2016). Acknowledging the findings of such research can facilitate the decisions people with dyslexia make about their future choices. In an empirical study of successful adults, Gerber et al. (1992) found the overriding factor to be the element to which they had been able to take control of their lives or felt in charge, dominating their situation rather than allowing themselves to be dominated by it. Control was seen to involve two sets of distinct but interrelated and interacting factors: internal decisions, that is, conscious decisions about taking control of one's life; external manifestations, that is, being able to adapt and shape oneself to be able to move ahead. They embrace both the medical and social models of disability but acknowledge the interaction of the two.

Internal Decisions

- A desire to succeed: adults wish to be successful, and this could have been evident in childhood but sometimes develops later. It is often the reason why people seek advice and guidance. Many people with dyslexia present as being highly motivated, and this is often intrinsic rather than extrinsic.

- Goal orientation: a major theme of lifespan developmental psychology is the existence of the dream or vision of life's goals (Upton, 2011). We all need long-term and short-term goals. One of the roles of the professional is to assist in helping people establish clear and achievable goals. A long-term goal could be to enter a particular occupation, a short-term goal to gain the necessary qualifications. When working with people who have a developmental disorder, it is important, however, to set even shorter-term goals, such as developing the literacy, learning, and technological skills appropriate to a course of training. Goals must be realistic and achievable; without establishing these they will not succeed.
- Reframing – sometimes called internal redeployment: this involves recognising that there are difficulties, accepting that they have strengths and weaknesses, and developing an understanding of their nature. It also refers to the process of reinterpreting the disability in productive and positive ways. It is 'a set of decisions relating to reinterpreting the learning disability in a more productive and positive manner. It clearly allows for one to identify strengths and parlay them into successful experiences, while still being aware of weakness that must be mitigated or bypassed' (Gerber et al., 1996, p. 98).

External Manifestations

- Persistence: this refers to a quality of determination. People show resilience, having experienced setbacks, but consider these to be an opportunity for learning and getting on with life. They show resolve, a willingness to make effort, and work hard.
- Learned creativity: this refers to strategy development. It is important that people with dyslexia address their problem with information processing, developing appropriate learning, memory, and metacognitive skills. They also need to find alternative ways of dealing with tasks, and the use of technology can be a significant factor.
- Goodness of fit: this is finding or creating environments in which it is possible to exploit strengths and succeed, and where one is comfortable with the demands, for example, being on the right course, at the right college, or in the right job.
- Social ecologies: this refers to the support systems people can rely on, such as colleagues, parents, partners, and supervisors. The positive role of supportive relationships has been a constant finding of research into success.

APPROACHES TO CAREER COUNSELLING AND DEVELOPMENT

Career development and counselling should be based on an idiographic approach to meet the unique needs of people with dyslexia. We all make career decisions within the context of a lifetime of experiences; we have expectations of work, so the exploration of intra-personal satisfaction they expect or derive from work is important. There is a need for skills-specific job selection, acquisition, and retention that need to be assessed or taught; there are personal, social, and environmental factors that need to be explored as these can be barriers to deciding on or pursuing a particular career (Wehman, 1996). Counsellers and clients should heed Stepehen Hawking, who wrote that his advice to other people with disabilities is to concentrate on things that their disability doesn't prevent them from doing well, and not regret the things that it interferes with (quoted in Dreifus, 2011).

We adopt a decision-making model based on that of Yost and Corbishley (1987), who argued that this has the advantage of focusing on the established core of career choice, that is, the centrality of decision making. They also suggested it has considerable face validity for clients and allows a good deal of flexibility. Their model consists of eight steps (outlined in McLoughlin & Leather, 2013), which were modified to address the needs of individuals with dyslexia. Here we expand on them further based on research into resilience and acknowledging that addressing working-memory difficulties should be central.

Step 1: Initial Assessment

The aim of this is to gather personal information about the client and to arrive at a sensible career-counselling goal they are interested in pursuing. The results of a diagnostic assessment should highlight abilities and perhaps strengths that might be relevant to a particular goal, ensuring that it is realistic. As we have written earlier, the competencies shown by the results of an assessment using tests such as the Wechsler Scales enables one to understand strengths and weaknesses, which can help people make optimal decisions about current and future careers, education, and training. It is worth repeating the comment made by Shaywitz et al. (2016) cited earlier in this book that self-awareness and self-knowledge, gained by an accurate diagnosis of dyslexia, bring in the light and allow the person to understand themself, to know how they function and learn, the nature of their difficulties, and how to help themself. There is no point in encouraging individuals to attempt courses or pursue occupations for which they have no aptitude, so dispelling erroneous beliefs based on the myths surrounding dyslexia is important here. Potential is a much-overused word as it often just refers to the academic, whereas factors such as personality are important in making career choices. Someone might have the intellectual abilities that enable them to succeed with medical training, but if they do not have good social skills, becoming a practising doctor is probably not a good choice.

Step 2: Self-Understanding

This involves helping the client to explore their values, interests, experience, and abilities that relate to their goals. This is when the process of reframing is important, as self-understanding is fundamental to effective goal setting. They need to develop their understanding of the impact having lower working-memory capacity might have on their performance and consider what this might mean in terms of achieving their goals.

Step 3: Making Sense of Self-Understanding Data

This entails synthesising information into a coherent set of statements that shows the desired outcomes for a career choice. Potential barriers to success in pursuing the desired career presented by dyslexia can be summarised. Career advisors should make themselves familiar with the language and implications of developmental disorders and know how to interpret diagnostic evaluations. Experience of success in education, training, and work can provide insights. The compensatory coping mechanisms hypothesis would suggest that individuals might have developed effective strategies they can draw upon.

Step 4: Generating Alternatives

Without making a judgement about the value of different options, a list of possible career alternatives is generated based on competencies and interests.

Step 5: Obtaining Occupational Information

This involves finding out about each option so an informed choice can be made. The list of options can be reduced by considering how lower working-memory capacity might undermine performance in an occupation or work environment. The cognitive load, intrinsic, extrinsic, and germane, that each might present should be considered.

Step 6: Making the Choice

The client makes a choice amongst options, the focus being on goodness of fit and the type of work environment that might suit them, so they are considering extrinsic overload. What options are open in terms of enabling the skills and strategies that address intrinsic overload? The early choice hypothesis would suggest that some young people have already established this for themselves and should be encouraged to be confident in their decisions.

Step 7: Making Plans to Reach the Career Choice Goal

Sometimes people don't achieve their short-term goals, so they need to have a plan B should this be the case. Alternative pathways can enable people to achieve their long-term goals, so contingency plans are worked out to handle setbacks, again considering possible demand on cognitive load and how this might be addressed. Sometimes the seemingly less direct route through coursework-evaluated, vocational, or apprentice programmes can ultimately lead to achieving the long-term goal.

Step 8: Implementing Plans

Short-term goals are addressed such as ensuring they have the literacy and technological strategies they require, that is, the learned creativities. The compensatory coping mechanisms hypothesis might suggest this is already the case, but people should be encouraged to have confidence in their way of working. They also need to learn how to present themselves in person to prospective employers. This includes how to disclose their disability in a constructive fashion.

DISCLOSURE

A risk facing individuals with dyslexia is being misunderstood, which raises the matter of disclosure, that is, telling employers, managers, and colleagues that they have a developmental disorder. If they are to access resources and accommodations, an individual must disclose that they have dyslexia, as well when they start applying for training courses, but they need to consider it carefully. One of the ways in which the success of disability legislation and the understanding of difficulties is reflected in society is the disclosure rate, that is, the extent to which individuals inform employers and colleagues that they have a learning difficulty. Research has suggested that individuals with learning disorders are reluctant to disclose, despite the existence of legislation that is supposed to prevent discrimination. In fact, many seem to fear discrimination, and hesitancy contributes to non-cognitive states such as low self-esteem (Nalavany et al., 2015). Studies have shown that most adults with dyslexia do not ask for accommodations or adjustments in the selection process, do not tell employers during interviews, and often do not ask for adjustments in a job (Madaus et al., 2002; Gerber & Price, 2003, 2008; Gerber et al., 2004). In our own follow-up study of graduates who had been allowed adjustments during their time at university (Martin & McLoughlin, 2012), some of the reasons given for not disclosing reflect much misunderstanding surrounding dyslexia, both in terms of the stereotypes held by people as well as the lack of understanding people with dyslexia have of themselves. Cited in McLoughlin & Leather (2013, p. 267), these included:

- 'I never thought it would apply to work.'
- 'I was afraid to be found out – they might have taken the job away.'
- 'They would think I couldn't do the job.'
- 'People would look down on you.'
- 'I was embarrassed.'
- 'I didn't think it was my place to ask for those things.'
- 'I would feel like a burden if they gave me anything extra.'

Most of these quotes reflect fear and anxiety about discrimination. The last two suggest that people who have developmental disorders do not seek to advantage themselves by requesting accommodations. They are just asking to be judged on their abilities, persistence, determination, and to be treated equally. Accommodations do not give extra knowledge, talent, or abilities. They just allow people to show that they can do the job. Having said that, it is essential that people with dyslexia are realistic about what they can achieve. They do need to have most of the competencies required; otherwise, no amount of accommodation can make up the difference. The underlying philosophy of disability legislation is integration. Too many accommodations can lead to isolation as well as a great deal of frustration and stress. 'Goodness of fit' is essential to success (Gerber et al., 1992). Disclosure, although a complex issue and process, is fundamental to achieving this. When it is undertaken positively, it should ensure that employers are able to meet a person's needs. Being able to 'disclose' in a constructive manner, providing solutions not problems and promoting one's skills, reflecting self-awareness and the ability to define oneself as more than one's disability, is one of the keys to success (Goldberg et al., 2003).

The hidden nature of dyslexia means that people have greater choice over whether to disclose (Gerber & Price, 2008). As it is a 'hidden disability', people must often advocate for themselves, their difficulties being less obvious and less well understood. Many find it a difficult issue, and research has revealed that people are reluctant to do so, fearing discrimination, but if they wish to access resources and be protected under the terms of legislation, they must. Snowling et al. (2012) found a strong tendency for fathers, parents with higher education qualifications, to self-report as dyslexic. They proposed that adults with higher educational qualifications who have relatively mild difficulties may see themselves as more handicapped in the workplace than their peers and hence be more likely to disclose than a similarly affected person in a manual job (Snowling et al., 2012).

Once they have self-understanding, the greatest expertise on the impact of dyslexia can come from the individual themselves. They are aware of its day-to-day effects and often have a good idea of how they work best. Few employers are experts in dyslexia, and this can apply to their human resources departments. Disclosure is an exercise in self-advocacy but involves educating others to avoid both positive and negative stereotypes. It can be an exercise in de-mythification, so people need to develop their understanding of themselves and how dyslexia might affect them in the workplace. 'I have dyslexia' is not enough; it leaves others to define it, usually based just on their experience of other people they have encountered. Individuals need to explain what it means to them and offer solutions. We suggest statements such as:

- 'Can I tell you what I think tomorrow as I need to read this thoroughly?'
- 'I can say things better than I can write or type them, so I like to use voice recognition software.'
- 'I get close to what I have written so don't always pick up my own mistakes, so I like to have others check over my work.'
- 'I like to be given instructions in writing as well as verbally.'
- 'I will remember who you are because I never forget a face.'

We get what we need by saying what we need, not by telling others that we have a problem. As we have written earlier, people need to be able to advocate for themselves based upon their self-understanding and individual differences. Without that, they fall victim to the positive and negative stereotypes held by the uninformed and the poorly informed. Having a developmental learning disorder should not prevent people from succeeding in life, but to just focus on that can raise expectations and lead to failure.

A decision-making approach to career counselling and guidance based on knowing the potential limitations placed on individuals by their inefficient working-memory capacity can foster self-understanding. It can also ensure that goals are realistic and achievable. It can help achieve the 'goodness of fit' essential to success, and effective disclosure, which might be complex, is fundamental to this. When it is undertaken positively, it should ensure that educational institutions and employers are able to meet a person's needs.

SUMMARY

In this chapter we have raised the issues that arise for career development if we understand dyslexia in the context of an inefficient working-memory system.

- We have described the important issues in differentiating between career guidance for those with dyslexia and those without.
- There has been reference to the need to avoid stereotyping and myths.
- The importance of addressing transitions in life has been considered.
- A decision-making model, based in self-understanding, that might underlie career guidance and development has been outlined.
- The importance of constructive disclosure to establish goodness of fit has been emphasised.

Conclusion

In this book we have attempted to draw together strands of research evidence and practice within psychological science to explain what dyslexia is and how its effects can be mitigated. We have noted that much of the research in the field has focused on children and their difficulties with learning to read and spell (Chapter 1). We wanted to focus on dyslexia as a lifelong condition that persists into adulthood and affects people's experiences in education, employment, and their social lives.

We consider that dyslexia is real, and both its underlying causes and effects can be measured (Chapter 2). Those wanting to assign a philosophical perspective to this approach might call it positivist or critical realist, though we believe the metaphorical self-flagellation of metaphysical discourse is not helpful when trying to help people with dyslexia understand their experiences. Dyslexia is *caused* by a relative deficit in working memory, and this can be measured using modern neurocognitive assessments such as the range of Wechsler tests. The *effects* of this relative deficit in working memory manifest as difficulties with information processing; this is often measured using literacy skill assessments but can also impact other domains of skill development. It is only by investigating this discrepancy between cognitive abilities (strengths and weaknesses, particularly in working memory) and other pertinent skills that dyslexia can be identified and diagnosed.

We have presented evidence to support the deficit in working memory in a sample of client data (Chapter 3). This shows a significant deficit in working memory in a selected sample of the population, adults reporting to a central London practice for a dyslexia assessment. Many of these people had been pre-screened, and there is no reason to believe they are representative of the general population. However, they are probably as representative of the population of adults with dyslexia in higher education or employment as can be achieved without mandatory assessment of everyone. This data demonstrates that these people were generally high in verbal knowledge and understanding but low in verbal information processing. It is this discrepancy that identifies them as dyslexic. At the individual level they will show a much greater variety of cognitive abilities and skill levels, which will have been emphasised in discussion with them and resulting assessment reports. However, at the population level this deficit in working memory and, to some extent, processing speed is strong and noteworthy.

It is important, then, to consider where working memory fits within the structures of memory more broadly (Chapter 4). Working memory (within the Baddeley model) is used for information processing. It has multiple components: a part for processing sounds (phonological loop), a part for processing visual information (visuo-spatial sketchpad), a part for directing attention and coordination (central executive) and a part for integrating information and bridging to long-term memory (episodic buffer). A later addition was the hedonic detection system that helps regulate emotional responses in the context of information processing. There may be different types of dyslexia characterised by which element of the working-memory system is deficient. It is understood that the phonological loop (the part for processing sounds) is important for learning to read (decode text) and write (encode text). For example, most people with dyslexia who struggle with spelling will have a relative deficit in phonological processing. However, people with dyslexia who have difficulty with executive functioning may be misdiagnosed as having ADD/ADHD if the appropriate assessments are not conducted and properly interpreted.

Rapid automatic naming (RAN) has been identified as an important measure linked to literacy development (Chapter 5). It can be conceptualised as a measure that links working-memory processing with long-term memory because the process of having to name stimuli quickly puts pressure on the ability to process information in working memory (phonological loop and episodic buffer) by linking visual stimuli (for example, colours, objects, digits, and letters) with their associated and well-established concepts in long-term memory. Rapid-naming assessments do not prima facie appear to be memory tests, because people tend to think these involve necessary recall (i.e. a word list or even a pub quiz). However, the benefit of the rapid-naming assessments is that they assess the processing within working memory by forcing the link to long-term memory and overloading the system in a way that the digit span test (in the WAIS and WISC) does not. Those who struggle with rapid naming will make a greater number of errors in assessments or, more commonly, slow their responses to free up the phonological loop and episodic buffer. Lower rapid-naming ability can help us to understand some of the difficulties that people with dyslexia report with tasks such as remembering people's names and left–right confusion.

The effect of these difficulties – deficit in working memory and the interaction between working memory and long-term memory – can be cognitive overload (Chapters 6 and 7). Working memory has a limited capacity even before we may encounter difficulties with processing, so it is prone to overload. The recognition that people with dyslexia are more susceptible to overload than their peers in education, the workplace, and everyday life is central to understanding how people can begin to help themselves and how others can assist them. Our view is that only by understanding that cognitive overload is one of the main manifestations of the experience of dyslexia can people with dyslexia begin to work through this limitation and start to succeed (Chapter 8). The development of effective strategies for working, whether in education or the workplace, is key to the person with dyslexia taking control of their own solutions. Strategy development will only be effective if the person is intrinsically motivated to learn and use new strategies. While they can be taught, they will not be effective if they are dictated by others. In addition, it should be acknowledged that there is no single strategy that works for everyone. When considering strategies to employ, the key question asked should be, 'what tends to cause cognitive overload for me?'

Those who wish to help people with dyslexia need to be aware of cognitive overload so that they can properly advise their clients (Chapter 8). They need to use general counselling skills to listen to their clients and interpret their experiences of cognitive overload (their phenomenology of dyslexia) and help them to actively analyse these experiences within the model of working-memory deficit and cognitive overload. The effective counsellor or coach will help the client to find and develop their own strategies that fit the kind of information they need to process in their context (e.g. education, employment, and/or social life). The counsellor's role here is to help their client to develop their own solutions so that they feel owned by the client and have long-lasting and pervasive benefits. Simply instructing clients, presenting one-size-fits-all solutions, or blaming metaphysical 'structures' or 'systems of oppression' will only reinforce their clients' feelings of failure and defeat in the long term, even if they are convenient external loci for the counsellor to explain why their client may not be 'progressing' when using ineffective interventions. We also believe that the use and integration of technology into strategy development is vital. Many modern technological solutions, whether these are mobile devices, such as cloud-linked smartphones, or software applications, such as voice recognition and LLM AI. To this end, counsellors and coaches must have an appreciation of the technology available and how to make it accessible to people with dyslexia. Clients who report that they do not like or use technology should be assisted with this because it will likely be the result of prior negative experiences with learning or using older technology that would have caused these reactions. The counsellor's job is, therefore, to use all means possible to help their client work through their cognitive overload by helping them to develop new strategies while exploring cognitive, behavioural, and emotional barriers to doing so.

Finally, those with dyslexia need to be able to adapt to transitional changes throughout their lives (Chapter 9). These are most evident in the transition from full-time education to the workplace, most commonly during the adolescent developmental period. However, transitions occur at other times in life, such as when changing jobs, or, more impactfully, changing careers, forming long-term relationships with others, parenting children, engaging in community service, and retiring from full-time employment. It is important that the person with dyslexia and those who live and work with them recognise that their vulnerability to cognitive overload will manifest in different ways in different contexts. If they can get ahead of these situations and recognise what may be coming, particularly what may be most difficult for them, it will result in a greater goodness of fit for them between their abilities, skills, and the context they find themselves in. This better fit will result in a more satisfactory, effective, and, hopefully, successful life experience for them. They will have available to them a range of strategies to work through their dyslexia. They will feel ownership over these strategies and have a greater feeling of self-efficacy. They will be able to use existing technological and future solutions to their advantage. They will do this because they have a greater understanding of and control over the things that are likely to cause them cognitive overload.

Appendix

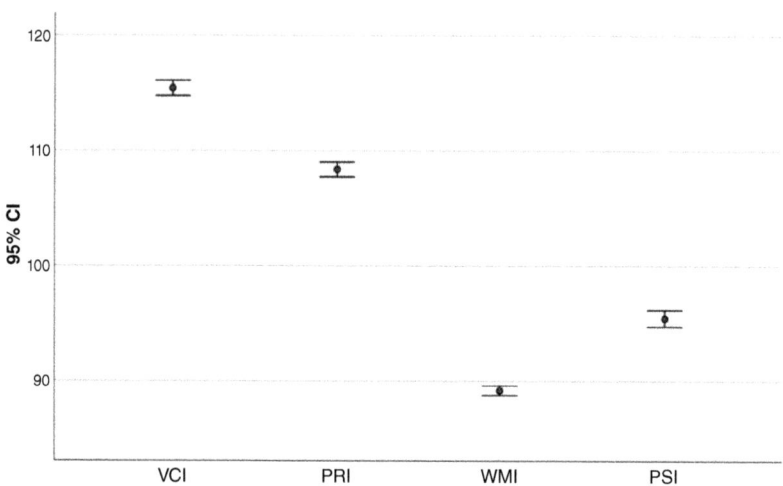

FIGURE A.1 Mean index scores for the Chapter 3 sample (with 95% CI).

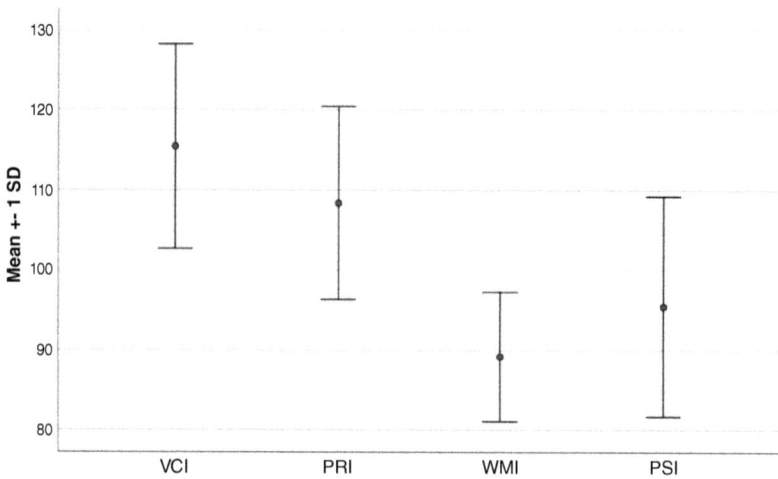

FIGURE A.2 Mean WAIS index scores for the Chapter 3 sample (with one standard deviation error range).

APPENDIX 145

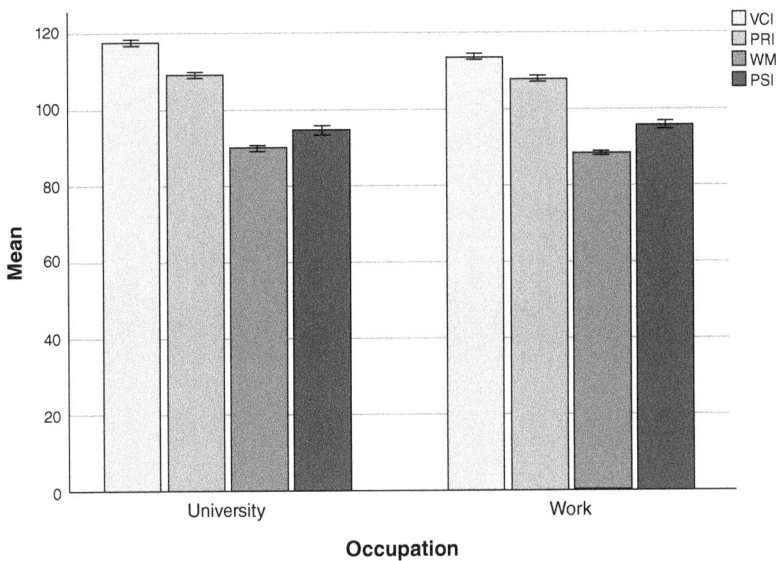

FIGURE A.3 Bar charts showing the mean index scores by client type, those in higher education (university) and those in employment (with 95% CI).

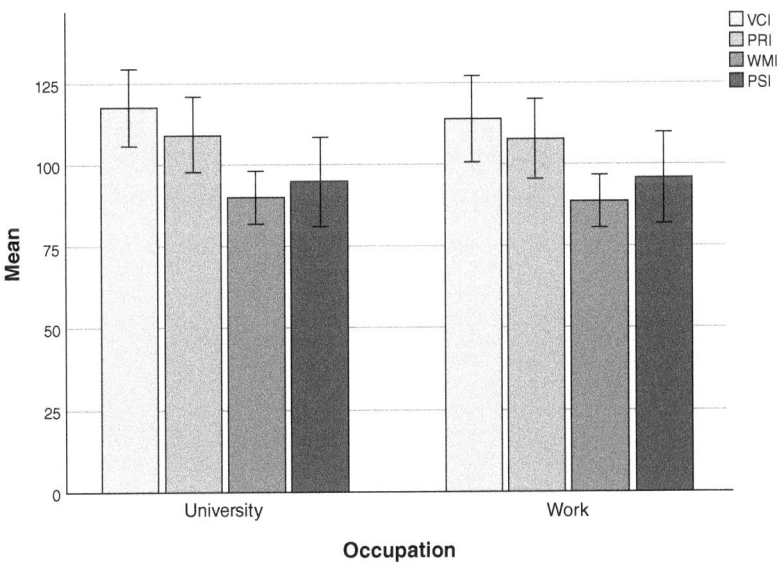

FIGURE A.4 Bar charts showing the mean index scores by client type, those in higher education (university) and those in employment (1 SD).

FIGURE A.5 Bar charts showing the mean subtest scores by client type, those in higher education (university) and those in employment (work). The error bars depict standard deviations.

Table A.1 Statistical appendices.

	Sex * Employment interaction	Sex main effect	Employment main effect
Similarities	$F = 1.16, p = .282$	$F = 11.05, p < .001$ ($= .007$)	$F = 53.67, p < .001$ ($= .033$)
Vocabulary	$F = 68.27, p = .002$ ($= .006$)	$F = 96.99, p < .001$ ($= .009$)	$F = 81.71, p < .001$ ($= .008$)
Information	$F = 3.17, p = .075$ ($= .002$)	$F = 43.72, p < .001$ ($= .027$)	$F = 5.61, p = .018$ ($= .004$)
Block design	$F = .06, p = .812$	$F = 21.06, p < .001$ ($= .013$)	$F = .18, p = .669$
Matrix reasoning	$F = .21, p = .649$	$F = 2.57, p = .109$	$F = 3.45, p = .064$
Visual puzzles	$F = 1.51, p = .219$	$F = 19.09, p < .001$ ($= .012$)	$F = .36, p = .547$
Digit span	$F = .19, p = .665$	$F = 8.07, p = .005$ ($= .005$)	$F = 7.09, p = .008$ ($= .005$)
Letter–number sequencing	$F = 1.92, p = .307$	$F = 2.16, p = .279$	$F = 1.54, p = .361$
Symbol search	$F = .87, p = .350$	$F = 14.43, p < .001$ ($= .009$)	$F = 4.21, p = .040$ ($= .003$)
Coding	$F = 1.19, p = .275$	$F = 14.89, p < .001$ ($= .010$)	$F = .57, p = .451$

Table A.1 (cont.)

	Sex * Employment interaction	Sex main effect	Employment main effect
Verbal comprehension	**F = 4.06, p = .044** (= .003)	**F = 27.66, p < .001** (= .018)	**F = 22.54, p < .001** (= .014)
Perceptual reasoning	F = .63, p = .428	**F = 22.66, p < .001** (= .014)	F = 1.73, p = .189
Working memory	F = .04, p = .837	**F = 7.40, p = .007** (= .005)	**F = 8.37, p = .004** (= .005)
Processing speed	F = .43, p = .512	**F = 14.32, p < .001** (= .009)	F = .88, p = .349

The significant findings ($p < .05$) are in **bold**, and the partial eta squared () effect sizes are shown below the significant effects.

References

Abbott-Jones, A. (2021). A quantitative study identifying the prevalence of anxiety in dyslexic students in higher education. *Research Journal of Education, 7*(1), 42–55.

Ackerman, P. L., Beier, M. E., & Boyle, M. D. (2002). Individual differences in working memory within a nomological network of cognitive and perceptual speed abilities. *Journal of Experimental Psychology: General, 131*(4), 567–589. https://doi.org/10.1037/0096-3445.131.4.567

Alexander-Passe, N. (2010). *Dyslexia and creativity: Investigations from differing perspectives.* Nova Science Publishers.

American Psychiatric Association. (2000). *Diagnostic and statistical manual of mental disorders* (4th ed., text rev., DSM-IV-TR). American Psychiatric Association.

American Psychiatric Association. (2009). *Wechsler Memory Scale* (4th ed.). American Psychiatric Association.

Amtmann, D., Abbott, R. D., & Berninger, V. W. (2007). Mixture growth models of RAN and RAS row by row: Insight into the reading system at work over time. *Reading and Writing, 20*(8), 785–813. https://doi.org/10.1007/s11145-006-9041-y

Anastasiou, D. (2024). Promoting science in specific learning disabilities: Three kinds of challenges. *IJRLD: International Journal for Research in Learning Disabilities, 7*(1), Article 1. https://doi.org/10.28987/ijrld.7.1.3

Araújo, S., & Faísca, L. (2019). A meta-analytic review of naming-speed deficits in developmental dyslexia. *Scientific Studies of Reading, 23*(5), 349–368. https://doi.org/10.1080/10888438.2019.1572758

Armstrong, T. (2015). The myth of the normal brain: Embracing neurodiversity. *AMA Journal of Ethics, 17*(4), 348–352. https://doi.org/10.1001/journalofethics.2015.17.4.msoc1-1504

Arthur, P., Khuu, S., & Blom, D. (2021). Visual processing abilities associated with piano music sight-reading expertise. *Psychology of Music, 49*(4), 1006–1016. https://doi.org/10.1177/0305735620920370

Astle, D. E., & Fletcher-Watson, S. (2020). Beyond the core-deficit hypothesis in developmental disorders. *Current Directions in Psychological Science, 29*(5), 431–437. https://doi.org/10.1177/0963721420925518

Auden, W. H. (2005). *W. H. Auden poems (selected by John Fuller)*. Faber & Faber.
Baddeley, A. (1986). *Working memory*. Clarendon Press/Oxford University Press.
Baddeley, A. (1992). Working memory. *Science, 255*(5044), 556–559. https://doi.org/10.1126/science.1736359
Baddeley, A. (2000). The episodic buffer: A new component of working memory? *Trends in Cognitive Sciences, 4*(11), 417–423. https://doi.org/10.1016/S1364-6613(00)01538-2
Baddeley, A. (2007). *Working memory, thought, and action* (Vol. 45). Oxford University Press.
Baddeley, A. (2010). Working memory. *Current Biology, 20*(4), R136–R140. https://doi.org/10.1016/j.cub.2009.12.014
Baddeley, A. D., & Hitch, G. J. (2007). Working memory: Past, present ... and future. In N. Osaka, R. H. Logie, & M. D'Esposito (Eds.), *The cognitive neuroscience of working memory* (pp. 1–20). Oxford University Press.
Baddeley, A. D., & Logie, R. H. (1999). Working memory: The multiple-component model. In A. Miyake & P. Shah (Eds.), *Models of working memory: Mechanisms of active maintenance and executive control* (pp. 28–61). Cambridge University Press. https://doi.org/10.1017/CBO9781139174909.005
Baddeley, A., Banse, R., Huang, Y. M., & Page, M. (2012). Working memory and emotion: Detecting the hedonic detector. *Journal of Cognitive Psychology, 24*(1), 6–16.
Baltes, P. B. (1987). Theoretical propositions of life-span developmental psychology: On the dynamics between growth and decline. *Developmental Psychology, 23*(5), 611.
Baltes, P. B., & Freund, A. M. (2003). Human strengths as the orchestration of wisdom and selective optimization with compensation. In L. G. Aspinwall & U. M. Staudinger (Eds.), *A psychology of human strengths: Fundamental questions and future directions for a positive psychology* (pp. 23–35). American Psychological Association. https://doi.org/10.1037/10566-002
Bannatyne, A. (1974). Diagnosis: A note on recategorization of the WISC scaled scores. *Journal of Learning Disabilities, 7*, 272–274.
Barquero, L. A., & Cutting, L. E. (2021). Introduction to the special issue on advances in the understanding of reading comprehension deficits. *Annals of Dyslexia, 71*(2), 211–217. https://doi.org/10.1007/s11881-021-00234-0
Beaulieu, C., Yip, E., Low, P. B., Mädler, B., Lebel, C. A., Siegel, L., Mackay, A. L., & Laule, C. (2020). Myelin water imaging demonstrates lower brain myelination in children and adolescents with poor reading ability. *Frontiers in Human Neuroscience, 14*, 1–12. https://doi.org/10.3389/fnhum.2020.568395
Beck, J. S. (2020). *Cognitive behavior therapy: Basics and beyond*. Guilford Press.

Benarroch, E. E. (2021). *Neuroscience for clinicians: Basic processes, circuits, disease mechanisms, and therapeutic implications*. Oxford University Press.

Boets, B., Op De Beeck, H. P., Vandermosten, M., Scott, S. K., Gillebert, C. R., Mantini, D., Bulthé, J., Sunaert, S., Wouters, J., & Ghesquière, P. (2013). Intact but less accessible phonetic representations in adults with dyslexia. *Science, 342*(6163), 1251–1254. https://doi.org/10.1126/science.1244333

Boyle, J. R. (2006). Learning from lectures: The implications of note-taking for students with learning disabilities. *Learning Disabilities: A Multidisciplinary Journal, 14*(2), 91–97.

Boyle, J. R. (2007). The process of note taking: Implications for students with mild disabilities. *The Clearing House: A Journal of Educational Strategies, Issues and Ideas, 80*(5), 227–232. https://doi.org/10.3200/TCHS.80.5.227-232

Brachacki, G. Z. W., Nicolson, R. I., & Fawcett, A. J. (1995). Impaired recognition of traffic signs in adults with dyslexia. *Journal of Learning Disabilities, 28*(5), 297–301. https://doi.org/10.1177/002221949502800505

Bradshaw, A. R., Woodhead, Z. V. J., Thompson, P. A., & Bishop, D. V. M. (2021). Profile of language abilities in a sample of adults with developmental disorders. *Dyslexia, 27*(1), 3–28. https://doi.org/10.1002/dys.1672

Breznitz, Z. (2008). The origin of dyslexia: The asynchrony phenomenon. In G. Reid, F. Manis, & A. Fawcett (Eds.), *The Sage handbook of dyslexia* (pp. 11–30). Sage.

Broadbent, H., & Mareschal, D. (2020). Neuroconstructivism. In *The encyclopedia of child and adolescent development* (pp. 1–11). John Wiley & Sons. https://doi.org/10.1002/9781119171492.wecad104

Brosnan, M., Demetre, J., Hamill, S., Robson, K., Shepherd, H., & Cody, G. (2002). Executive functioning in adults and children with developmental dyslexia. *Neuropsychologia, 40*(12), 2144–2155.

Brunswick, N., & Bargary, S. (2022). Self-concept, creativity and developmental dyslexia in university students: Effects of age of assessment. *Dyslexia, 28*(3), 293–308. https://doi.org/10.1002/dys.1722

Callens, M., Tops, W., Stevens, M., & Brysbaert, M. (2014). An exploratory factor analysis of the cognitive functioning of first-year bachelor students with dyslexia. *Annals of Dyslexia, 64*(1), 91–119. https://doi.org/10.1007/s11881-013-0088-6

Cameron, H. (2024). 'It's been taken away': An experience of a disappearing dyslexia diagnosis. *International Journal of Inclusive Education, 28*(1), 1–15. https://doi.org/10.1080/13603116.2021.1902003

Carawan, L. W., Nalavany, B. A., & Jenkins, C. (2016). Emotional experience with dyslexia and self-esteem: The protective role of perceived family support in late adulthood. *Aging & Mental Health, 20*(3), 284–294. https://doi.org/10.1080/13607863.2015.1008984

Carr, N. (2020). *The shallows: What the internet is doing to our brains.* W. W. Norton & Company.

Christodoulou, J. A., Del Tufo, S. N., Lymberis, J., Saxler, P. K., Ghosh, S. S., Triantafyllou, C., Whitfield-Gabrieli, S., & Gabrieli, J. D. (2014). Brain bases of reading fluency in typical reading and impaired fluency in dyslexia. *PLoS ONE, 9*(7), e100552.

Clark, D. A., & Beck, A. T. (2010). Cognitive theory and therapy of anxiety and depression: Convergence with neurobiological findings. *Trends in Cognitive Sciences, 14*(9), 418–424.

Connelly, V., Dockrell, J. E., & Barnett, J. (2005). The slow handwriting of undergraduate students constrains overall performance in exam essays. *Educational Psychology, 25*(1), 99–107. https://doi.org/10.1080/0144341042000294912

Constantinidis, C., & Klingberg, T. (2016). The neuroscience of working memory capacity and training. *Nature Reviews Neuroscience, 17*(7), 438–449.

Cowan, N. (2012). *Working memory capacity.* Psychology Press.

Critchley, M. (1981). Dyslexia: An overview. In G. Pavlidis & T. Miles R. (Eds.), *Dyslexia: Research and its application to education* (pp. 1–11). John Wiley & Sons.

Crowe, S. F. (2000). Does the letter number sequencing task measure anything more than digit span? *Assessment, 7*(2), 113–117. https://doi.org/10.1177/107319110000700202

Damasio, A. R. (1996). The somatic marker hypothesis and the possible functions of the prefrontal cortex. *Philosophical Transactions of the Royal Society of London. Series B: Biological Sciences, 351*(1346), 1413–1420. https://doi.org/10.1098/rstb.1996.0125

Davelaar, E. J. (2013). Short-term memory as a working memory control process. *Frontiers in Psychology, 4*, 13.

David, D., Cristea, I., & Hofmann, S. G. (2018). Why cognitive behavioral therapy is the current gold standard of psychotherapy. *Frontiers in Psychiatry, 9*, 4.

Deacon, L., Macdonald, S. J., & Donaghue, J. (2022). 'What's wrong with you, are you stupid?' Listening to the biographical narratives of adults with dyslexia in an age of 'inclusive' and 'anti-discriminatory' practice. *Disability & Society, 37*(3), 406–426. https://doi.org/10.1080/09687599.2020.1815522

Deacon, T. W. (1998). *The symbolic species: The co-evolution of language and the brain.* W. W. Norton & Company.

Démonet, J. F., Taylor, M. J., & Chaix, Y. (2004). Developmental dyslexia. *The Lancet*, *363*(9419), 1451–1460.

D'Mello, A. M., & Gabrieli, J. D. E. (2018). Cognitive neuroscience of dyslexia. *Language, Speech, and Hearing Services in Schools*, *49*(4), 798–809. https://doi.org/10.1044/2018_LSHSS-DYSLC-18-0020

Doolittle, P. (2013, June). How your 'working memory' makes sense of the world. *TED*.

Doust, C., Fontanillas, P., Eising, E., Gordon, S. D., Wang, Z., Alagöz, G., Molz, B., & Pourcain, B. S. (2022). Discovery of 42 genome-wide significant loci associated with dyslexia. *Nature Genetics*, *54*(11), 1621–1629.

Doyle, N. (2020). Neurodiversity at work: A biopsychosocial model and the impact on working adults. *British Medical Bulletin*, *135*(1), 108–125.

Doyle, N. E., & McDowall, A. (2019). Context matters: A review to formulate a conceptual framework for coaching as a disability accommodation. *PLoS ONE*, *14*(8), e0199408.

Dreifus, C. (2011, 9 May). Life and the cosmos, word by painstaking word. *The New York Times*. www.nytimes.com/2011/05/10/science/10hawking.html

Dyslexia Foundation (2016). *Beyond a reading disability: Examining the full spectrum of abilities/disabilities of the unique dyslexic brain*. Dyslexia Foundation. https://dyslexiafoundation.org/beyond-a-reading-disability-examining-the-full-spectrum-of-abilitiesdisabilities-of-the-unique-dyslexic-brain/

Einstein, G. O., & McDaniel, M. A. (2005). Prospective memory: Multiple retrieval processes. *Current Directions in Psychological Science*, *14*(6), 286–290.

Elliott, J. G., & Grigorenko, E. L. (2014). *The dyslexia debate*. Cambridge University Press.

Elliott, J. G., & Grigorenko, E. L. (2024). *The dyslexia debate revisited*. Cambridge University Press.

Ellis, A. (1962). *Reason and emotion in psychotherapy*. Lyle Stuart.

Eloranta, A. K., Närhi, V. M., Eklund, K. M., Ahonen, T. P., & Aro, T. I. (2019). Resolving reading disability: Childhood predictors and adult-age outcomes. *Dyslexia*, *25*(1), 20–37.

Ericsson, K. A., & Chase, W. G. (1982). Exceptional memory: Extraordinary feats of memory can be matched or surpassed by people with average memories that have been improved by training. *American Scientist*, *70*(6), 607–615.

Evans, R. J. W. (2020). A pioneer in context: T. R. Miles and the Bangor dyslexia unit. *Oxford Review of Education*, *46*(4), 439–453.

Faust, M., & Sharfstein-Friedman, S. (2003). Naming difficulties in adolescents with dyslexia: Application of the tip-of-the-tongue paradigm. *Brain and Cognition*, *53*(2), 211–217.

Ferrari, J. R., & Díaz-Morales, J. F. (2007). Perceptions of self-concept and self-presentation by procrastinators: Further evidence. *The Spanish Journal of Psychology, 10*(1), 91–96.

Ferreira, É. de M. R., Pinto, R. Z., Arantes, P. M. M., Vieira, É. L. M., Teixeira, A. L., Ferreira, F. R., & Vaz, D. V. (2020). Stress, anxiety, self-efficacy, and the meanings that physical therapy students attribute to their experience with an objective structured clinical examination. *BMC Medical Education, 20*, 1–9.

Fiorello, C. A., Flanagan, D. P., & Hale, J. B. (2014). The utility of the pattern of strengths and weaknesses approach. *Learning Disabilities, 20*, 55–59.

Frith, U. (1999). Paradoxes in the definition of dyslexia. *Dyslexia, 5*(4), 192–214. https://doi.org/10.1002/(SICI)1099-0909(199912)5:4<192::AID-DYS144>3.0.CO;2-N

Fuster, J. M. (1997). *The prefrontal cortex*. Raven.

Galaburda, A. M., & Kemper, T. L. (1979). Cytoarchitectonic abnormalities in developmental dyslexia: A case study. *Annals of Neurology, 6*(2), 94–100. https://doi.org/10.1002/ana.410060203

Galaburda, A. M., Sherman, G. F., Rosen, G. D., Aboitiz, F., & Geschwind, N. (1985). Developmental dyslexia: Four consecutive patients with cortical anomalies. *Annals of Neurology, 18*(2), 222–233. https://doi.org/10.1002/ana.410180210

Georgiou, G. K., Martinez, D., Vieira, A. P. A., Antoniuk, A., Romero, S., & Guo, K. (2022). A meta-analytic review of comprehension deficits in students with dyslexia. *Annals of Dyslexia, 72*(2), 204–248. https://doi.org/10.1007/s11881-021-00244-y

Gerber, P. J., & Price, L. A. (2003). Persons with learning disabilities in the workplace: What we know so far in the Americans with Disabilities Act era. *Learning Disabilities Research & Practice, 18*(2), 132–136. https://doi.org/10.1111/1540-5826.00069

Gerber, P. J., & Price, L. A. (2008). Self-disclosure and adults with learning disabilities: Practical ideas about a complex process. *Learning Disabilities: A Multidisciplinary Journal, 15*(1), 21–24.

Gerber, P. J., Ginsberg, R., & Reiff, H. B. (1992). Identifying alterable patterns in employment success for highly successful adults with learning disabilities. *Journal of Learning Disabilities, 25*(8), 475–487. https://doi.org/10.1177/002221949202500802

Gerber, P. J., Reiff, H. B., & Ginsberg, R. (1996). Reframing the learning disabilities experience. *Journal of Learning Disabilities, 29*(1), 98–101. https://doi.org/10.1177/002221949602900112

Gerber, P. J., Price, L. A., Mulligan, R., & Shessel, I. (2004). Beyond transition: A comparison of the employment experiences of American and Canadian adults with LD. *Journal of Learning Disabilities, 37*(4), 283–291. https://doi.org/10.1177/00222194040370040101

Gibbs, S. J., & Elliott, J. G. (2020). The dyslexia debate: Life without the label. *Oxford Review of Education, 46*(4), 487–500. https://doi.org/10.1080/03054985.2020.1747419

Gilger, J. W., & A Special Topics Panel of the Dyslexia Foundation (TDF). (2017). Beyond a reading disability: Comments on the need to examine the full spectrum of abilities/disabilities of the atypical dyslexic brain. *Annals of Dyslexia, 67*(2), 109–113. https://doi.org/10.1007/s11881-017-0142-x

Glazzard, J. (2015). A critical analysis of learning styles and multiple intelligences and their contribution to inclusive education. *Journal of Global Research in Education and Social Science, 2*(3), 107–113.

Gleichgerrcht, E., Fridriksson, J., & Bonilha, L. (2015). Neuroanatomical foundations of naming impairments across different neurologic conditions. *Neurology, 85*(3), 284–292. https://doi.org/10.1212/wnl.0000000000001765

Goldberg, R. J., Higgins, E. L., Raskind, M. H., & Herman, K. L. (2003). Predictors of success in individuals with learning disabilities: A qualitative analysis of a 20-year longitudinal study. *Learning Disabilities Research & Practice, 18*(4), 222–236. https://doi.org/10.1111/1540-5826.00077

Goller, H., Banks, J. B., & Meier, M. E (2020). An individual differences investigation of the relations among life event stress, working memory capacity, and mind wandering: A preregistered replication-extension study. *Memory & Cognition, 48*(5), 759–771. https://doi.org/10.3758/s13421-020-01014-8

Gregg, N. (2014). *Adults with learning disabilities: Factors contributing to persistence*. In H. L. Swanson, K. R. Harris, & S. Graham (Eds.), *Handbook of learning disabilities* (2nd ed., pp. 85–103). Guilford Press.

Groeger, J. A. (1997). *Memory and remembering: Everyday memory in context*. Addison Wesley Longman.

Grondin, S. (Ed.). (2008). *Psychology of time*. Emerald Group Publishing.

Guyer, P., & Wood, A. W. (1998). *Critique of pure reason (the Cambridge Edition of the Works of Immanuel Kant)*. Cambridge University Press.

Habib, M. (2021). The neurological basis of developmental dyslexia and related disorders: A reappraisal of the temporal hypothesis, twenty years on. *Brain Sciences, 11*(6), 708.

Hacker, P. M. S. (2017). *The passions: A study of human nature*. John Wiley & Sons.

Hagoort, P. (2017). The core and beyond in the language-ready brain. *Neuroscience & Biobehavioral Reviews, 81*, 194–204.

Harris, K. M., & McDade, T. W. (2018). The biosocial approach to human development, behavior, and health across the life course. *RSF: The Russell Sage Foundation Journal of the Social Sciences, 4*(4), 2–26.

Harrison, A. G., Pollock, B., & Holmes, A. (2022). Provision of extended assessment time in post-secondary settings: A review of the literature and proposed guidelines for practice. *Psychological Injury and Law, 15*(3), 295–306. https://doi.org/10.1007/s12207-022-09451-3

Hayes, S. C., Strosahl, K. D., & Wilson, K. G. (2011). *Acceptance and commitment therapy: The process and practice of mindful change.* Guilford Press.

Herbert, D. M. B., & Burt, J. S. (2004). What do students remember? Episodic memory and the development of schematization. *Applied Cognitive Psychology, 18*(1), 77–88. https://doi.org/10.1002/acp.947

Hong, H. V., & Hong, E. H. (Eds.). (2000). *The essential Kierkegaard.* Princeton University Press.

Huettig, F., Lachmann, T., Reis, A., & Petersson, K. M. (2018). Distinguishing cause from effect: Many deficits associated with developmental dyslexia may be a consequence of reduced and suboptimal reading experience. *Language, Cognition and Neuroscience, 33*(3), 333–350. https://doi.org/10.1080/23273798.2017.1348528

Isaacs, C. (2019). *Adult dyslexia: Unleashing your limitless power.* Cheryl Isaacs.

Jankowski, T., & Holas, P. (2020). Effects of brief mindfulness meditation on attention switching. *Mindfulness, 11*, 1150–1158.

Jodrell, D. (2010). Social-identity and self-efficacy concern for disability labels. *Psychology Teaching Review, 16*(2), 111–121.

Kahana, M. J., Aggarwal, E. V., & Phan, T. D. (2018). The variability puzzle in human memory. *Journal of Experimental Psychology: Learning, Memory, and Cognition, 44*(12), 1857.

Kahneman, D., Sibony, O., & Sunstein, C. R. (2021). *Noise: A flaw in human judgment.* Hachette UK.

Karmiloff-Smith, A. (1994). Précis of Beyond modularity: A developmental perspective on cognitive science. *Behavioral and Brain Sciences, 17*(4), 693–707.

Kauffman, J. M. (2007). Labels and the nature of special education: We need to face realities. *Learning Disabilities: A Multidisciplinary Journal, 14*(4), 245–248.

Kauffman, J. M., & Sasso, G. M. (2006). Rejoinder: Certainty, doubt, and the reduction of uncertainty. *Exceptionality, 14*(2), 109–120. https://doi.org/10.1207/s15327035ex1402_4

Kirk, S. A. (1962). *Educating exceptional children.* Houghton Mifflin.

Kirsh, D. (2000). A few thoughts on cognitive overload. *Intellectica Revue de l Association pour la Recherche Cognitive, 30*(1), 19–51.

Klassen, R. (2002). A question of calibration: A review of the self-efficacy beliefs of students with learning disabilities. *Learning Disability Quarterly, 25*(2), 88–102.

Klingberg, T. (2009). *The overflowing brain: Information overload and the limits of working memory*. Oxford University Press.

Knight, B. A., & Galletly, S. (2020). Practical school-level implications of cognitive processing and cognitive load. In A. M. Columbus (Ed.), *Advances in psychology research* (Vol. 140, pp. 1–90). Nova Science Publishers.

Krcmar, K., & Horsman, T. (2014). *Mindfulness for study: From procrastination to action*. Inspired by Learning.

Leather, C., Hogh, H., Seiss, E., & Everatt, J. (2011). Cognitive functioning and work success in adults with dyslexia. *Dyslexia, 17*(4), 327–338. https://doi.org/10.1002/dys.441

Lee, J. J., McGue, M., Iacono, W. G., Michael, A. M., & Chabris, C. F. (2019). The causal influence of brain size on human intelligence: Evidence from within-family phenotypic associations and GWAS modeling. *Intelligence, 75*, 48–58.

Levitin, D. J. (2014). *Organized mind: Thinking straight in the age of information overload*. Barnes & Noble.

Lewandowski, L. J., Berger, C., Lovett, B. J., & Gordon, M. (2016). Test-taking skills of high school students with and without learning disabilities. *Journal of Psychoeducational Assessment, 34*(6), 566–576. https://doi.org/10.1177/0734282915622854

Lewis, R. B. (1998). Assistive technology and learning disabilities: Today's realities and tomorrow's promises. *Journal of Learning Disabilities, 31*(1), 16–26. https://doi.org/10.1177/002221949803100103

Lezak, M. D., Howieson, D. B., Bigler, E. D., & Tranel, D. (2012). *Neuropsychological assessment*. Oxford University Press.

Lichtenberger, E. O., & Kaufman, A. S. (2012). *Essentials of WAIS-IV assessment*. John Wiley & Sons.

Lipton, P. (2017). Inference to the best explanation. In H. Newton-Smith (Ed.), *A companion to the philosophy of science* (2nd ed., pp. 184–193). John Wiley and Sons. https://doi.org/10.1002/9781405164481.ch29

Lisica, D., Koso-Drljević, M., Stürmer, B., Džubur, A., & Valt, C. (2022). Working memory impairment in relation to the severity of anxiety symptoms. *Cognition and Emotion, 36*(6), 1093–1108. https://doi.org/10.1080/02699931.2022.2081535

Logan, J. (2009). Dyslexic entrepreneurs: The incidence; their coping strategies and their business skills. *Dyslexia, 15*(4), 328–346. https://doi.org/10.1002/dys.388

Lyubomirsky, S. (2011). Hedonic adaptation to positive and negative experiences. In S. Folkman (Ed.), *The Oxford handbook of stress, health, and coping* (pp. 200–222). Oxford University Press.

Macdonald, K., Germine, L., Anderson, A., Christodoulou, J., & McGrath, L. M. (2017). Dispelling the myth: Training in education or neuroscience decreases but does not eliminate beliefs in neuromyths. *Frontiers in Psychology, 8*, 1314.

Madaus, J. W., Foley, T. E., McGuire, J. M., & Ruban, L. M. (2002). Employment self-disclosure of postsecondary graduates with learning disabilities: Rates and rationales. *Journal of Learning Disabilities, 35*(4), 364–369. https://doi.org/10.1177/00222194020350040701

Marsiske, M., Lang, F. R., Baltes, P. B., & Baltes, M. M. (1995). Selective optimization with compensation: Life-span perspectives on successful human development. In R. A. Dixon & L. Backman (Eds.), *Compensating for psychological deficits and declines: Managing losses and promoting gains* (pp. 35–79). Lawrence Erlbaum Associates.

Martin, A., & McLoughlin, D. (2012). Disclosing dyslexia: An exercise in self-advocacy. In N. Brunswick (Ed.), *Supporting dyslexic adults in higher education and the workplace* (1st ed., pp. 123–135). John Wiley and Sons. https://doi.org/10.1002/9781119945000.ch13

Masten, A. S. (2001). Ordinary magic: Resilience processes in development. *American Psychologist, 56*(3), 227.

Maughan, B., Messer, J., Collishaw, S., Pickles, A., Snowling, M., Yule, W., & Rutter, M. (2009). Persistence of literacy problems: Spelling in adolescence and at mid-life. *Journal of Child Psychology and Psychiatry, 50*(8), 893–901. https://doi.org/10.1111/j.1469-7610.2009.02079.x

Mazur-Mosiewicz, A., & Davis, A. S. (2011). Rapid automized naming. In S. Goldstein & J. A. Naglieri (Eds.), *Encyclopedia of child behavior and development* (pp. 1212–1213). Springer US. https://doi.org/10.1007/978-0-387-79061-9_2335

McAdams, D. P. (2011). Narrative identity. In S. J. Schwartz, K. Luyckx, & V. L. Vignoles (Eds.), *Handbook of identity theory and research* (pp. 99–115). Springer. https://doi.org/10.1007/978-1-4419-7988-9_5

McCrory, E. J., Mechelli, A., Frith, U., & Price, C. J. (2005). More than words: A common neural basis for reading and naming deficits in developmental dyslexia? *Brain, 128*(2), 261–267.

McGilchrist, I. (2019). *The master and his emissary: The divided brain and the making of the Western world.* Yale University Press.

McLoughlin, D. (2018). Dyslexia and transitions. *Perspectives on Language and Literacy, 44*, 7–8.

McLoughlin, D., & Leather, C. (2013). *The dyslexic adult: Interventions and outcomes – an evidence-based approach.* John Wiley & Sons.

McLoughlin, D., Fitzgibbon, G., & Young, V. (1994). *Adult dyslexia: Assessment, counselling and training*. Whurr.

Melby-Lervåg, M., & Hulme, C. (2013). Is working memory training effective? A meta-analytic review. *Developmental Psychology*, *49*(2), 270.

Melby-Lervåg, M., Redick, T. S., & Hulme, C. (2016). Working memory training does not improve performance on measures of intelligence or other measures of 'far transfer': Evidence from a meta-analytic review. *Perspectives on Psychological Science*, *11*(4), 512–534. https://doi.org/10.1177/1745691616635612

Miles, T. R. (1983). *Dyslexia: The pattern of difficulties*. Granada.

Miles, T. R., Haslum, M. N., & Wheeler, T. J. (1998). Gender ratio in dyslexia. *Annals of Dyslexia*, *48*(1), 27–55. https://doi.org/10.1007/s11881-998-0003-8

Milton, D. (2019). Disagreeing over neurodiversity. *Psychologist*, *32*, 8.

Momaday, N. S. (1987). *The names: A memoir* (Vol. 16). University of Arizona Press.

Moojen, S. M. P., Gonçalves, H. A., Bassôa, A., Navas, A. L., De Jou, G., & Miguel, E. S. (2020). Adults with dyslexia: How can they achieve academic success despite impairments in basic reading and writing abilities? The role of text structure sensitivity as a compensatory skill. *Annals of Dyslexia*, *70*(1), 115–140. https://doi.org/10.1007/s11881-020-00195-w

Moran, T. P. (2016). Anxiety and working memory capacity: A meta-analysis and narrative review. *Psychological Bulletin*, *142*(8), 831.

Nalavany, B. A., Carawan, L. W., & Rennick, R. A. (2011). Psychosocial experiences associated with confirmed and self-identified dyslexia: A participant-driven concept map of adult perspectives. *Journal of Learning Disabilities*, *44*(1), 63–79. https://doi.org/10.1177/0022219410374237

Nalavany, B. A., Carawan, L. W., & Sauber, S. (2015). Adults with dyslexia, an invisible disability: The mediational role of concealment on perceived family support and self-esteem. *The British Journal of Social Work*, *45*(2), 568–586.

Nicolson, R. I., & Fawcett, A. J. (1990). Automaticity: A new framework for dyslexia research? *Cognition*, *35*(2), 159–182.

Nicolson, R. I., & Fawcett, A. J. (1995). Dyslexia is more than a phonological disability. *Dyslexia*, *1*, 19–36.

Nicolson, R. I., & Fawcett, A. J. (2019). Development of dyslexia: The delayed neural commitment framework. *Frontiers in Behavioral Neuroscience*, *13*, 112.

Norton, E. S., Beach, S. D., & Gabrieli, J. D. (2015). Neurobiology of dyslexia. *Current Opinion in Neurobiology*, *30*, 73–78.

Oberauer, K., Farrell, S., Jarrold, C., & Lewandowsky, S. (2016). What limits working memory capacity? *Psychological Bulletin*, *142*(7), 758.

O'Brien, D. (1993). *How to develop a perfect memory.* Lybrary.com.

Odegard, T. N., & Dye, M. (2024). The gift of dyslexia: What is the harm in it? *Annals of Dyslexia, 74*(2), 143–157. https://doi.org/10.1007/s11881-024-00308-9

Oefinger, L. M., & Peverly, S. T. (2020). The lecture note-taking skills of adolescents with and without learning disabilities. *Journal of Learning Disabilities, 53*(3), 176–188. https://doi.org/10.1177/0022219419897268

Olsen, J. (2024). Employers: Influencing disabled people's employment through responses to reasonable adjustments. *Disability & Society, 39*(3), 791–810. https://doi.org/10.1080/09687599.2022.2099251

Papadopoulos, T. C. (2023). William M. Cruickshank Memorial Lecture: New directions in the study of neurodevelopmental disorders. *IJRLD: International Journal for Research in Learning Disabilities, 6*(1), 3–13.

Parker, H. (2022). *Hybrid humans: Dispatches from the frontiers of man and machine.* Profile Books.

Pathak, V. C. (2017). Phenomenological research: A study of lived experiences. *International Journal of Advance Research and Innovative Ideas in Education, 3*(1), 1719–1722.

Patterson, E. E., & Kahan, T. A. (2020). Precrastination and the cognitive-load-reduction (CLEAR) hypothesis. *Memory, 28*(1), 107–111. https://doi.org/10.1080/09658211.2019.1690001

Peavler, J. (2024). The gatekeeper of learning. *Perspectives on Language and Literacy, 50*(2), 16–20.

Pengelley, J., Whipp, P. R., & Malpique, A. (2025). A testing load: A review of cognitive load in computer and paper-based learning and assessment. *Technology, Pedagogy and Education, 34*(1), 1–17. https://doi.org/10.1080/1475939X.2024.2367517

Pennington, B. F., McGrath, L. M., Peterson, R., & Peterson, R. L. (2019). *Diagnosing learning disorders: From science to practice.* Guilford Press.

Pinker, S. (2003). *The blank slate: The modern denial of human nature.* Penguin.

Pinker, S. (2015). *The sense of style: The thinking person's guide to writing in the 21st century.* Penguin.

Pinker, S. (2022). *Rationality: What it is, why it seems scarce, why it matters.* Penguin.

Piotrowska, B., & Barratt, J. (2024). Investigating low intelligence stereotype threat in adults with developmental dyslexia. *Dyslexia, 30*(2), e1766. https://doi.org/10.1002/dys.1766

Popper, K. R. (1963). *Conjectures and refutations.* Routledge and Kegan Paul.

Price, L., & Patton, J. (2002). Reshuffling the puzzle pieces: Connecting adult developmental theory to learning disabilities. *Career Planning and Adult Development Journal, 18*(1), 10–48.

Protopapa, C., & Smith-Spark, J. H. (2022). Self-reported symptoms of developmental dyslexia predict impairments in everyday cognition in adults. *Research in Developmental Disabilities, 128*, 104288.

Protopapas, A., & Parrila, R. (2018). Is dyslexia a brain disorder? *Brain Sciences, 8*(4), 61.

Ramus, F. (2014). Should there really be a 'dyslexia debate'? *Brain, 137*(12), 3371–3374.

Ramus, F., Altarelli, I., Jednoróg, K., Zhao, J., & Di Covella, L. S. (2018). Neuroanatomy of developmental dyslexia: Pitfalls and promise. *Neuroscience & Biobehavioral Reviews, 84*, 434–452.

Rauch, A., & Frese, M. (2000). Psychological approaches to entrepreneurial success: A general model and an overview of findings. *International Review of Industrial and Organizational Psychology, 15*, 101–142.

Redelmeier, D. A., Etchells, E. E., & Najeeb, U. (2025). Trusting in lived experience. *Journal of the Royal Society of Medicine, 118*(1), 5–10. https://doi.org/10.1177/01410768241288343

Reiff, H. B., Gerber, P. J., & Ginsberg, R. (1993). Definitions of learning disabilities from adults with learning disabilities: The insiders' perspectives. *Learning Disability Quarterly, 16*(2), 114–125. https://doi.org/10.2307/1511133

Reis, A., Araújo, S., Morais, I. S., & Faísca, L. (2020). Reading and reading-related skills in adults with dyslexia from different orthographic systems: A review and meta-analysis. *Annals of Dyslexia, 70*(3), 339–368. https://doi.org/10.1007/s11881-020-00205-x

Revelle, W., Wilt, J., & Rosenthal, A. (2010). Individual differences in cognition: New methods for examining the personality–cognition link. In A. Gruszka, G. Matthews, & B. Szymura (Eds.), *Handbook of individual differences in cognition* (pp. 27–49). Springer US. https://doi.org/10.1007/978-1-4419-1210-7_2

Rogelberg, S. G., Scott, C. W., Agypt, B., Williams, J., Kello, J. E., McCausland, T., & Olien, J. L. (2014). Lateness to meetings: Examination of an unexplored temporal phenomenon. *European Journal of Work and Organizational Psychology, 23*(3), 323–341. https://doi.org/10.1080/1359432X.2012.745988

Rogers, C. (1951). *Client-centered therapy*. Houghton Mifflin.

Rose, S. J. (2009). *Identifying and teaching children and young people with dyslexia and literacy difficulties: An independent report from Sir Jim Rose to the Secretary of State for Children, Schools and Families*. Department for Children, Schools and Families.

Rosenbaum, D. A., Fournier, L. R., Levy-Tzedek, S., McBride, D. M., Rosenthal, R., Sauerberger, K., VonderHaar, R. L., Wasserman, E. A., & Zentall, T. R. (2019). Sooner rather than later: Precrastination rather than procrastination. *Current*

Directions in Psychological Science, 28(3), 229–233. https://doi.org/10.1177/0963721419833652

Roth, A., Fonagy, P., Parry, G., Target, M., & Woods, R. (1996). *What works for whom? A critical review of psychotherapy research*. Guilford Press.

Rovelli, C. (2018). *Reality is not what it seems: The journey to quantum gravity*. Penguin.

Rozin, P., & Royzman, E. B. (2001). Negativity bias, negativity dominance, and contagion. *Personality and Social Psychology Review, 5*(4), 296–320. https://doi.org/10.1207/S15327957PSPR0504_2

Runswick-Cole, K. (2014). 'Us' and 'them': The limits and possibilities of a 'politics of neurodiversity' in neoliberal times. *Disability & Society, 29*(7), 1117–1129. https://doi.org/10.1080/09687599.2014.910107

Russell, G. (2020). Critiques of the neurodiversity movement. In S. Kapp (Ed.), *Autistic community and the neurodiversity movement* (pp. 287–303). Palgrave Macmillan.

Sagan, C., & Druyan, A. (1997). *The demon-haunted world: Science as a candle in the dark*. Ballantine Books.

Sandi, C. (2013). Stress and cognition. *WIREs Cognitive Science, 4*(3), 245–261. https://doi.org/10.1002/wcs.1222

Sartre, J.-P. (1971). *Sketch for a theory of the emotions*. Routledge.

Satel, S., & Lilienfeld, S. O. (2013). *Brainwashed: The seductive appeal of mindless neuroscience*. Basic Civitas Books.

Scerri, E. M., & Will, M. (2023). The revolution that still isn't: The origins of behavioral complexity in Homo sapiens. *Journal of Human Evolution, 179*, 103358.

Schnieders, C. A., Gerber, P. J., & Goldberg, R. J. (2015). Integrating findings of studies of successful adults with learning disabilities: A new comprehensive model for researchers and practitioners. *Career Planning & Adult Development Journal, 31*(4), 99–110.

Schweizer, S., Satpute, A. B., Atzil, S., Field, A. P., Hitchcock, C., Black, M., Barrett, L. F., & Dalgleish, T. (2019). The impact of affective information on working memory: A pair of meta-analytic reviews of behavioral and neuroimaging evidence. *Psychological Bulletin, 145*(6), 566.

Scott, R., (2004). *Dyslexia and counselling*. Whurr.

Seidenberg, M. (2017). *Language at the speed of sight: How we read, why so many cannot, and what can be done about it*. Basic Books.

Shakespeare, T. (2013). *Disability rights and wrongs revisited*. Routledge.

Shaywitz, B. A., Weiss, L. G., Saklofske, D. H., & Shaywitz, S. E. (2016). Translating scientific progress in dyslexia into twenty-first century diagnosis and interventions. WISC-V assessment and interpretation: Scientist-practitioner perspectives. In L. G. Weiss, D. H. Saklofske, J. A. Holdnack, & A. Prifitera (Eds.), *Practical resources for the mental health professional* (pp. 269–286). Academic Press.

Shermer, M. (2018). *Heavens on earth: The scientific search for the afterlife, immortality, and utopia*. Henry Holt.

Shinaver, C. S., Entwistle, P. C., & Söderqvist, S. (2014). Cogmed WM training: Reviewing the reviews. *Applied Neuropsychology: Child*, 3(3), 163–172. https://doi.org/10.1080/21622965.2013.875314

Shura, R. D., Hurley, R. A., & Taber, K. H. (2016). Working memory models: Insights from neuroimaging. *The Journal of Neuropsychiatry and Clinical Neurosciences*, 28(1), A4–A5. https://doi.org/10.1176/appi.neuropsych.15120402

Siegel, L. S. (2019). Solving the problem of learning disabilities. *IJRLD: International Journal for Research in Learning Disabilities*, 4(1), 3–11.

Siegel, L. S., Hurford, D. P., Metsala, J., & Odegard, T. N. (2022). The demise of the discrepancy definition of dyslexia: Commentary on Snowling, Hulme, and Nation. *IJRLD: International Journal for Research in Learning Disabilities*, 5(2), 49–54.

Smith-Spark, J., Fawcett, A., Nicolson, R., & Fisk, J. (2004). Dyslexic students have more everyday cognitive lapses. *Memory*, 12(2), 174–182. https://doi.org/10.1080/09658210244000450

Smith-Spark, J. H., & Fisk, J. E. (2007). Working memory functioning in developmental dyslexia. *Memory*, 15(1), 34–56. https://doi.org/10.1080/09658210601043384

Smith-Spark, J. H., Henry, L. A., Messer, D. J., Edvardsdottir, E., & Zięcik, A. P. (2016). Executive functions in adults with developmental dyslexia. *Research in Developmental Disabilities*, 53, 323–341.

Snowling, M., Dawes, P., Nash, H., & Hulme, C. (2012). Validity of a protocol for adult self-report of dyslexia and related difficulties. *Dyslexia*, 18(1), 1–15. https://doi.org/10.1002/dys.1432

Snowling, M. J. (2014). Dyslexia: A language learning impairment. *Journal of the British Academy*, 2(1), 43–58.

Snowling, M. J., Hulme, C., & Nation, K. (2020). Defining and understanding dyslexia: Past, present and future. *Oxford Review of Education*, 46(4), 501–513. https://doi.org/10.1080/03054985.2020.1765756

Spadafore, G. J. (1983). *SDRT: Spadafore diagnostic reading test manual*. Academic Therapy Publications.

Spekman, N. J., Goldberg, R. J., & Herman, K. L. (1992). Learning disabled children grow up: A search for factors related to success in the young adult years.

Learning Disabilities Research & Practice, 7(3), 161–170. https://doi.org/10.1177/093889829200700308

Steele, C. M., & Aronson, J. (1995). Stereotype threat and the intellectual test performance of African Americans. *Journal of Personality and Social Psychology, 69*(5), 797.

Stein, J. (2023). Theories about developmental dyslexia. *Brain Sciences, 13*(2), 208.

Swanson, H. L. (2015). Intelligence, working memory, and learning disabilities. In T. C. Papadopoulos, R. K. Parrila, & J. R. Kirby (Eds.), *Cognition, intelligence, and achievement: A tribute to J. P. Das* (pp. 175–196). Academic Press.

Swanson, H. L., & Hsieh, C.-J. (2009). Reading disabilities in adults: A selective meta-analysis of the literature. *Review of Educational Research, 79*(4), 1362–1390. https://doi.org/10.3102/0034654309350931

Sweller, J. (1988). Cognitive load during problem solving: Effects on learning. *Cognitive Science, 12*(2), 257–285.

Sweller, J. (2011). Cognitive load theory. In *Psychology of learning and motivation* (Vol. 55, pp. 37–76). Elsevier.

Sweller, J. (2019). Human problem solving and instructional design. In H. Askell-Williams & J. Orrell (Eds.), *Problem solving for teaching and learning* (pp. 25–33). Routledge.

Symons, C. S., & Johnson, B. T. (1997). The self-reference effect in memory: A meta-analysis. *Psychological Bulletin, 121*(3), 371.

Tallis, R. (2009). NEURO TRASH. *New Humanist, 124*(6), 18.

Tanner, K. (2009). Adult dyslexia and the 'conundrum of failure'. *Disability & Society, 24*(6), 785–797. https://doi.org/10.1080/09687590903160274

Tarrasch, R., Berman, Z., & Friedmann, N. (2016). Mindful reading: Mindfulness meditation helps keep readers with dyslexia and ADHD on the lexical track. *Frontiers in Psychology, 7*, 578.

Trautmann, M. (2014). A neuroconstructivistic research strategy to study the underlying causes of dyslexia. *Translational Developmental Psychiatry, 2*(1), 21684. https://doi.org/10.3402/tdp.v2.21684

Tremblay, P., & Dick, A. S. (2016). Broca and Wernicke are dead, or moving past the classic model of language neurobiology. *Brain and Language, 162*, 60–71.

Tulving, E. (2001). Episodic memory and common sense: How far apart? *Philosophical Transactions of the Royal Society of London. Series B: Biological Sciences, 356*(1413), 1505–1515. https://doi.org/10.1098/rstb.2001.0937

Tulving, E. (2002). Episodic memory: From mind to brain. *Annual Review of Psychology, 53*(1), 1–25. https://doi.org/10.1146/annurev.psych.53.100901.135114

Turner, M. (2008). *Psychological assessment of dyslexia*. John Wiley & Sons.

Upton, T. (2011). Forensic rehabilitation services in the United States: Contemporary status and future directions. *Psicología, Conocimiento y Sociedad, 1*(4), 41–51.

VonderHaar, R. L., McBride, D. M., & Rosenbaum, D. A. (2019). Task order choices in cognitive and perceptual-motor tasks: The cognitive-load-reduction (CLEAR) hypothesis. *Attention, Perception, & Psychophysics, 81*(7), 2517–2525. https://doi.org/10.3758/s13414-019-01754-z

Von Karolyi, C., Winner, E., Gray, W., & Sherman, G. F. (2003). Dyslexia linked to talent: Global visual-spatial ability. *Brain and Language, 85*(3), 427–431.

Vorontsova-Wenger, O., Ghisletta, P., Ababkov, V., Bondolfi, G., & Barisnikov, K. (2022). Short mindfulness-based intervention for psychological and academic outcomes among university students. *Anxiety, Stress, & Coping, 35*(2), 141–157. https://doi.org/10.1080/10615806.2021.1931143

Wagner, R. K., Torgesen, J. K., Rashotte, C. A & Pearson, N. A. (1999). Comprehensive test of phonological processing: CTOPP. Austin, TX: Pro-ed.

Wagner, R. K., Torgesen, J. K., & Rashotte, C. A. (2013). *Comprehensive test of phonological processing (CTOPP)* (2nd ed.). PRO-ED.

Wampold, B. E. (2013). *The great psychotherapy debate: Models, methods, and findings*. Routledge.

Warmington, M., Stothard, S. E., & Snowling, M. J (2012). Assessing dyslexia in higher education: The York adult assessment battery revised. *Journal of Research in Special Educational Needs*, 7–14. https://doi.org/10.1111/j.1471-3802.2012.01264.x

Wechsler, D. (2010). *Wechsler adult intelligence scale* (4th ed., technical and interpretive manual). Pearson Assessment.

Wechsler, D. (2017). *Wechsler individual achievement test* (3rd ed., WIAT-III UK). Pearson Assessment.

Wechsler, D. (2024). *Wechsler adult intelligence scale* (5th ed., WAIS-V, administration and scoring manual). Pearson Assessment.

Wechsler, D., Coalson, D. L., & Raiford, S. E. (2008). *WAIS-IV: Wechsler adult intelligence scale* (Vol. 10). Pearson.

Wehman, P. (1996). Transition into postsecondary education. *Journal of Vocational Rehabilitation, 6*(3), 209–211.

Weisberg, D. S., Keil, F. C., Goodstein, J., Rawson, E., & Gray, J. R. (2008). The seductive allure of neuroscience explanations. *Journal of Cognitive Neuroscience, 20*(3), 470–477.

West, S., King, V., Carey, T. S., Lohr, K. N., McKoy, N., Sutton, S. F., & Lux, L. (2002). Systems to rate the strength of scientific evidence: Summary. In *AHRQ evidence report summaries*. Agency for Healthcare Research and Quality (US).

Westermann, G., Mareschal, D., Johnson, M. H., Sirois, S., Spratling, M. W., & Thomas, M. S. C. (2007). Neuroconstructivism. *Developmental Science, 10*(1), 75–83. https://doi.org/10.1111/j.1467-7687.2007.00567.x

Wiig, E. H., Nielsen, N. P., & Jacobson, J. M. (2007). A quick test of cognitive speed: Patterns of age groups 15 to 95 years. *Perceptual and Motor Skills, 104*(3), 1067–1075. https://doi.org/10.2466/pms.104.4.1067-1075

Wilhelm, O., Hildebrandt, A., & Oberauer, K. (2013). What is working memory capacity, and how can we measure it? *Frontiers in Psychology, 4*, 433.

Wolf, M., & Bowers, P. G. (1999). The double-deficit hypothesis for the developmental dyslexias. *Journal of Educational Psychology, 91*(3), 415.

Wolf, M., Gotlieb, R. J. M., Kim, S. A., Pedroza, V., Rhinehart, L. V., Tempini, M. L. G., & Sears, S. (2024). Towards a dynamic, comprehensive conceptualization of dyslexia. *Annals of Dyslexia, 74*(3), 303–324. https://doi.org/10.1007/s11881-023-00297-1

Wolff, U., & Lundberg, I. (2002). The prevalence of dyslexia among art students. *Dyslexia, 8*(1), 34–42. https://doi.org/10.1002/dys.211

World Health Organization. (n.d.). *International Classification of Diseases (ICD)*. World Health Organization. www.who.int/standards/classifications/classification-of-diseases

Yan, B., & Zhang, X. (2022). What research has been conducted on procrastination? Evidence from a systematical bibliometric analysis. *Frontiers in Psychology, 13*, 809044.

Yost, E. B., & Corbishley, M. A. (1987). *Career counseling: A psychological approach*. Jossey-Bass.

Zaks, Z. (2024). Changing the medical model of disability to the normalization model of disability: Clarifying the past to create a new future direction. *Disability & Society, 39*(12), 3233–3260. https://doi.org/10.1080/09687599.2023.2255926

Zhu, J., & Weiss, L. (2005). The Wechsler scales. In *Contemporary intellectual assessment: Theories, tests, and issues* (pp. 297–324). Guilford Press.

Index

anxiety, 10, 14, 27, 41, 63, 74–75, 78, 93, 109, 113–114, 117–122, 127, 136
attention, 24, 26, 47, 67, 70, 72–74, 79, 101, 107, 109, 117, 121, 140
attribution theory, 117

career counselling, 123, 126, 128, 132, 138
career guidance, 32, 40, 128, 138
central executive, 70, 72, 85, 140
cerebellum, 23, 66, 77
cognitive behavioural therapy, 117–119
cognitive flexibility, 48
cognitive inefficiency, xii
cognitive load, 84, 88, 90, 93, 99, 101, 103, 108, 134
cognitive load theory, 87–89, 105, 107, 127
cognitive processing, 8, 88, 109
cognitive restructuring, 116
co-morbidity, 15
compensate, 89
compensation, 73, 96–98, 100, 105, 111
compensatory coping, 126, 134–135
connectivity, 25, 70, 85, 125
connectivity (brain), 10
counselling, 75, 112, 142

declarative (memory), 65–66
decoding, 5, 8–9
developmental dyslexia, 8, 20
digit span, 41, 47, 50–52, 55, 58, 61, 72, 91, 141
digit span (test), 17
disclosure, 135–138
dyschronia, 20, 102
dysnomia, 83, 85
dyspraxia, 15, 42

empathy, 29, 64, 112
encoding, 5
episodic buffer, 73, 101, 140–141
executive functions, 18, 26, 63, 69, 73, 75, 78, 87, 110

falsifiability, 6
fMRI, 23–24, 65, 125

hedonic adaptation, 73

individual differences, 32, 68–69, 110, 138
interventions, 13, 16, 34, 75, 91, 97, 113, 121, 142

long-term memory, 24, 66–67, 72–73, 76, 80, 88, 93, 113, 116, 118, 140–141
low self-esteem, 27, 89, 114, 135

memory strategies, 87, 92–93, 96
meta-cognitive skills, 101

negative valence, 74
neuroconstructivism, 24
neurodevelopmental, 4
neurodevelopmental disorders, 25, 27, 29, 55, 65, 69, 123, 129, xii
neurodiversity, 13, 30, 102, 120, 132
non-cognitive attributes, 27

phonological deficit, 71, 85
phonological loop, 70, 72–73, 79, 85, 102, 140–141
positive valence, 74
practitioner, 21
practitioner scientist, xi
prefrontal cortex, 77, 85
processing speed, 3–4, 17, 35, 38, 43, 45, 48, 50–51, 55, 58, 60, 63, 79, 81–82, 140

rapid automatic naming, 26, 80–82, 85
rational emotive therapy, 117
reading comprehension, 7, 19, 27–28, 36, 39, 70, 102, 107, 110
resilience, 129–132
retrieval, 23, 66, 71–73, 75, 79–80, 93–94

167

schema, 6, 15, 75, 88, 95, 97, 119
self-efficacy, 10, 98, 101, 114, 143
semantic memory, 67, 83, 92–94, 104–105
short-term memory, 18, 47, 65, 71, 94
skill development, 5, 77, 80, 86, 97–98, 100, 139
stress management, 121

technological aids, 105
transition, 126, 143
transition (occupational), 40

visual-spatial sketchpad, 70, 72–73

working-memory capacity, 11, 18, 67–68, 76, 87, 90, 96, 109, 126, 133–134, 138
working-memory model, 33, 128
working-memory network, 77

For EU product safety concerns, contact us at Calle de José Abascal, 56–1º, 28003 Madrid, Spain or eugpsr@cambridge.org.

www.ingramcontent.com/pod-product-compliance
Ingram Content Group UK Ltd.
Pitfield, Milton Keynes, MK11 3LW, UK
UKHW022026010426
469595UK00020B/383